YASIR ARAFAT

MENACHEM BEGIN

TONY BLAIR

GEORGE W. BUSH

JIMMY CARTER

FIDEL CASTRO

VICENTE FOX

SADDAM HUSSEIN

HAMID KARZAI

KIM IL SUNG AND KIM JONG IL

HOSNI MUBARAK

PERVEZ MUSHARRAF

VLADIMIR PUTIN

MOHAMMED REZA PAHLAVI

ANWAR SADAT

THE SAUDI ROYAL FAMILY

GERHARD SCHROEDER

ARIEL SHARON

Hamid Karzai

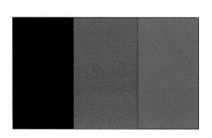

Anne M. Todd

CHELSEA HOUSE
PUBLISHERS
A Haights Cross Communications Company

CHELSEA HOUSE PUBLISHERS

V.P., New Product Development Sally Cheney
Director of Production Kim Shinners
Creative Manager Takeshi Takahashi
Manufacturing Manager Diann Grasse

Staff for HAMID KARZAI

Executive Editor Lee Marcott
Senior Editor Tara Koellhoffer
Production Assistant Megan Emery
Picture Research 21st Century Publishing and Communications, Inc.
Series and Cover Designer Takeshi Takahashi
Layout 21st Century Publishing and Communications, Inc.

A Haights Cross Communications ✦ Company

http://www.chelseahouse.com

First Printing

1 3 5 7 9 8 6 4 2

Library of Congress Cataloging-in-Publication Data

Todd, Anne M.
  Hamid Karzai / by Anne M. Todd.
      p. cm. -- (Major world leaders)
Summary: A biography of the man who, in December 2001, was selected to head an interim
government and lead Afghanistan toward peace and prosperity after many years of occupation, violence, and poverty. Includes bibliographical references and index.
  ISBN 0-7910-7649-0
  1. Karzai, Hamid--Juvenile literature. 2. Afghanistan--Politics and government--Juvenile
literature. 3. Presidents--Afghanistan--Biography--Juvenile literature. [1. Karzai, Hamid. 2.
Afghanistan--Politics and government. 3. Presidents--Afghanistan.] I. Title. II. Series.
  DS371.33.K37T64 2003
  958.104'6--dc21

                                                                                    2003013650

TABLE OF CONTENTS

On Leadership

Arthur M. Schlesinger, jr.

Leadership, it may be said, is really what makes the world go round. Love no doubt smoothes the passage; but love is a private transaction between consenting adults. Leadership is a public transaction with history. The idea of leadership affirms the capacity of individuals to move, inspire, and mobilize masses of people so that they act together in pursuit of an end. Sometimes leadership serves good purposes, sometimes bad; but whether the end is benign or evil, great leaders are those men and women who leave their personal stamp on history.

Now, the very concept of leadership implies the proposition that individuals can make a difference. This proposition has never been universally accepted. From classical times to the present day, eminent thinkers have regarded individuals as no more than the agents and pawns of larger forces, whether the gods and goddesses of the ancient world or, in the modern era, race, class, nation, the dialectic, the will of the people, the spirit of the times, history itself. Against such forces, the individual dwindles into insignificance.

So contends the thesis of historical determinism. Tolstoy's great novel *War and Peace* offers a famous statement of the case. Why, Tolstoy asked, did millions of men in the Napoleonic Wars, denying their human feelings and their common sense, move back and forth across Europe slaughtering their fellows? "The war," Tolstoy answered, "was bound to happen simply because it was bound to happen." All prior history determined it. As for leaders, they, Tolstoy said, "are but the labels that serve to give a name to an end and, like labels, they have the least possible connection with the event." The greater the leader, "the more conspicuous the inevitability and the predestination of every act he commits." The leader, said Tolstoy, is "the slave of history."

Determinism takes many forms. Marxism is the determinism of class. Nazism the determinism of race. But the idea of men and women as the slaves of history runs athwart the deepest human instincts. Rigid determinism abolishes the idea of human freedom—the assumption of free choice that underlies every move we make, every word we speak, every thought we think. It abolishes the idea of human responsibility, since it is manifestly unfair to reward or punish people for actions that are by definition beyond their control. No one can live consistently by any deterministic creed. The Marxist states prove this themselves by their extreme susceptibility to the cult of leadership.

More than that, history refutes the idea that individuals make no difference. In December 1931 a British politician crossing Fifth Avenue in New York City between 76th and 77th Streets around 10:30 P.M. looked in the wrong direction and was knocked down by an automobile— a moment, he later recalled, of a man aghast, a world aglare: "I do not understand why I was not broken like an eggshell or squashed like a gooseberry." Fourteen months later an American politician, sitting in an open car in Miami, Florida, was fired on by an assassin; the man beside him was hit. Those who believe that individuals make no difference to history might well ponder whether the next two decades would have been the same had Mario Constasino's car killed Winston Churchill in 1931 and Giuseppe Zangara's bullet killed Franklin Roosevelt in 1933. Suppose, in addition, that Lenin had died of typhus in Siberia in 1895 and that Hitler had been killed on the Western Front in 1916. What would the 20th century have looked like now?

For better or for worse, individuals do make a difference. "The notion that a people can run itself and its affairs anonymously," wrote the philosopher William James, "is now well known to be the silliest of absurdities. Mankind does nothing save through initiatives on the part of inventors, great or small, and imitation by the rest of us—these are the sole factors in human progress. Individuals of genius show the way, and set the patterns, which common people then adopt and follow."

Leadership, James suggests, means leadership in thought as well as in action. In the long run, leaders in thought may well make the greater difference to the world. "The ideas of economists and political philosophers, both when they are right and when they are wrong," wrote John Maynard Keynes, "are more powerful than is commonly understood. Indeed the world is ruled by little else. Practical men, who believe themselves to be quite exempt from any intellectual influences, are usually the slaves of some defunct economist. . . . The power of vested interests is vastly exaggerated compared with the gradual encroachment of ideas."

But, as Woodrow Wilson once said, "Those only are leaders of men, in the general eye, who lead in action. . . . It is at their hands that new thought gets its translation into the crude language of deeds." Leaders in thought often invent in solitude and obscurity, leaving to later generations the tasks of imitation. Leaders in action—the leaders portrayed in this series—have to be effective in their own time.

And they cannot be effective by themselves. They must act in response to the rhythms of their age. Their genius must be adapted, in a phrase from William James, "to the receptivities of the moment." Leaders are useless without followers. "There goes the mob," said the French politician, hearing a clamor in the streets. "I am their leader. I must follow them." Great leaders turn the inchoate emotions of the mob to purposes of their own. They seize on the opportunities of their time, the hopes, fears, frustrations, crises, potentialities. They succeed when events have prepared the way for them, when the community is awaiting to be aroused, when they can provide the clarifying and organizing ideas. Leadership completes the circuit between the individual and the mass and thereby alters history.

It may alter history for better or for worse. Leaders have been responsible for the most extravagant follies and most monstrous crimes that have beset suffering humanity. They have also been vital in such gains as humanity has made in individual freedom, religious and racial tolerance, social justice, and respect for human rights.

There is no sure way to tell in advance who is going to lead for good and who for evil. But a glance at the gallery of men and women in MAJOR WORLD LEADERS suggests some useful tests.

One test is this: Do leaders lead by force or by persuasion? By command or by consent? Through most of history leadership was exercised by the divine right of authority. The duty of followers was to defer and to obey. "Theirs not to reason why/Theirs but to do and die." On occasion, as with the so-called enlightened despots of the 18th century in Europe, absolutist leadership was animated by humane purposes. More often, absolutism nourished the passion for domination, land, gold, and conquest and resulted in tyranny.

The great revolution of modern times has been the revolution of equality. "Perhaps no form of government," wrote the British historian James Bryce in his study of the United States, *The American Commonwealth*, "needs great leaders so much as democracy." The idea that all people should be equal in their legal condition has undermined the old structure of authority, hierarchy, and deference. The revolution of equality has had two contrary effects on the nature of leadership. For equality, as Alexis de Tocqueville pointed out in his great study *Democracy in America*, might mean equality in servitude as well as equality in freedom.

"I know of only two methods of establishing equality in the political world," Tocqueville wrote. "Rights must be given to every citizen, or none at all to anyone . . . save one, who is the master of all." There was no middle ground "between the sovereignty of all and the absolute power of one man." In his astonishing prediction of 20th-century totalitarian dictatorship, Tocqueville explained how the revolution of equality could lead to the *Führerprinzip* and more terrible absolutism than the world had ever known.

But when rights are given to every citizen and the sovereignty of all is established, the problem of leadership takes a new form, becomes more exacting than ever before. It is easy to issue commands and enforce them by the rope and the stake, the concentration camp and the *gulag*. It is much harder to use argument and achievement to overcome opposition and win consent. The Founding Fathers of the United States understood the difficulty. They believed that history had given them the opportunity to decide, as Alexander Hamilton wrote in the first Federalist Paper, whether men are indeed capable of basing government on "reflection and choice, or whether they are forever destined to depend . . . on accident and force."

Government by reflection and choice called for a new style of leadership and a new quality of followership. It required leaders to be responsive to popular concerns, and it required followers to be active and informed participants in the process. Democracy does not eliminate emotion from politics; sometimes it fosters demagoguery; but it is confident that, as the greatest of democratic leaders put it, you cannot fool all of the people all of the time. It measures leadership by results and retires those who overreach or falter or fail.

It is true that in the long run despots are measured by results too. But they can postpone the day of judgment, sometimes indefinitely, and in the meantime they can do infinite harm. It is also true that democracy is no guarantee of virtue and intelligence in government, for the voice of the people is not necessarily the voice of God. But democracy, by assuring the right of opposition, offers built-in resistance to the evils inherent in absolutism. As the theologian Reinhold Niebuhr summed it up, "Man's capacity for justice makes democracy possible, but man's inclination to justice makes democracy necessary."

A second test for leadership is the end for which power is sought. When leaders have as their goal the supremacy of a master race or the promotion of totalitarian revolution or the acquisition and exploitation of colonies or the protection of greed and privilege or the preservation of personal power, it is likely that their leadership will do little to advance the cause of humanity. When their goal is the abolition of slavery, the liberation of women, the enlargement of opportunity for the poor and powerless, the extension of equal rights to racial minorities, the defense of the freedoms of expression and opposition, it is likely that their leadership will increase the sum of human liberty and welfare.

Leaders have done great harm to the world. They have also conferred great benefits. You will find both sorts in this series. Even "good" leaders must be regarded with a certain wariness. Leaders are not demigods; they put on their trousers one leg after another just like ordinary mortals. No leader is infallible, and every leader needs to be reminded of this at regular intervals. Irreverence irritates leaders but is their salvation. Unquestioning submission corrupts leaders and demeans followers. Making a cult of a leader is always a mistake. Fortunately hero worship generates its own antidote. "Every hero," said Emerson, "becomes a bore at last."

The signal benefit the great leaders confer is to embolden the rest of us to live according to our own best selves, to be active, insistent, and resolute in affirming our own sense of things. For great leaders attest to the reality of human freedom against the supposed inevitabilities of history. And they attest to the wisdom and power that may lie within the most unlikely of us, which is why Abraham Lincoln remains the supreme example of great leadership. A great leader, said Emerson, exhibits new possibilities to all humanity. "We feed on genius. . . . Great men exist that there may be greater men."

Great leaders, in short, justify themselves by emancipating and empowering their followers. So humanity struggles to master its destiny, remembering with Alexis de Tocqueville: "It is true that around every man a fatal circle is traced beyond which he cannot pass; but within the wide verge of that circle he is powerful and free; as it is with man, so with communities." ■

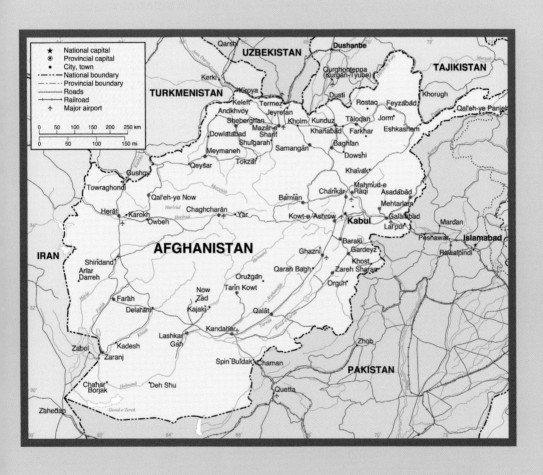

1

Hamid Karzai Takes the Challenge

When Hamid Karzai steps into a room, people take notice. He is carefully groomed and impeccably dressed. On his bald head, he wears a lamb's wool hat called a karakul. His mustache and beard are neatly trimmed. He wears an Afghan collarless tunic with matching loose trousers, together called a piran-tunban. Over the tunic he wears an elegant, tailored sportscoat. He sometimes wears a colorful traditional robe called a chapan, common in the Uzbek cultures of northern Afghanistan, over his sportscoat. Karzai is a mix of old and new customs. In 2002, Tom Ford, a designer from Gucci, called Karzai "the chicest man on the planet today." Hamid Karzai stands tall and proud, and his demeanor and clothes portray a man of intelligence and honor. Karzai is courageous, smart, funny, calm, and peaceful. People around the world admire him.

Karzai has not always felt such strong support and admiration.

In the 1980s, Karzai lived in exile in Pakistan, a neighbor of Afghanistan. While in Pakistan, he worked to stop the Soviet invasion of his homeland, Afghanistan. At that time, Afghans as well as people from the United States and other countries did not take Karzai very seriously. They considered him a scholarly individual—a person who would rather read about politics than be a part of them. Others thought Karzai might be too nice to quell the prolific violence in Afghanistan. Yet the more Karzai spoke in his calm, stately demeanor, the more people began to take notice and listen. He had dreams of a peaceful Afghanistan, one with a unified government and fair laws for all people.

Seen here addressing Afghanistan's Loya Jirga, or grand assembly, in June 2002, Hamid Karzai is known for his sharp sense of fashion as much as for his political skill.

In December 2001, Karzai was selected to lead an interim government for Afghanistan. Before this, Afghanistan had faced more than two decades of war: first, fighting the invading Soviet Union; then, enduring years of tribal infighting among Afghanistan's resistance fighters, the mujahideen; and finally, fighting Islamic extremists, the Taliban. The newly chosen Karzai faced an incredible challenge. He needed to bring peace to a country that had grown far too familiar with war. Karzai took the challenge in stride, however. With his relaxed disposition, his intelligence, and his willingness to listen to all sides of an issue, Karzai has been successful in bringing hope to a war-torn country.

2

Growing up in Afghanistan

A fghanistan is a landlocked country, surrounded by the countries of Uzbekistan, Tajikistan, Pakistan, Iran, and Turkmenistan. Many ethnic groups live in Afghanistan, but there are four major ones. From largest to smallest, they are the Pushtuns, the Tajiks, the Hazaras, and the Uzbeks. All except the Hazaras spill over into neighboring countries. The Pushtuns are also in Pakistan, the Tajiks in Tajikistan, and the Uzbeks in Uzbekistan. The Hazaras live in central Afghanistan in the mountains and valleys. They are thought to have arrived in Afghanistan in the thirteenth century, when Genghis Khan and his army came through. The Hazaras are descendants of his soldiers.

The Pushtuns make up between 40 percent and 60 percent of Afghans. They live mostly in southern and eastern Afghanistan. Within the Pushtun ethnic group, thousands of tribes exist. The

Afghanistan is a rugged country inhabited by many different ethnic groups. Many Afghans are residents of small villages, like these people who live outside of Baghran.

second largest ethnic group is the Tajiks. Although they can be found throughout Afghanistan, most of the people living in the northeast, near the border with Tajikistan, are Tajiks. About equal in number to the Hazaras are the Uzbeks. They speak a Turkish language and live in northern Afghanistan.

In 1992, Afghanistan became an Islamic state, meaning that the church and its religious leaders controlled the government's decisions. Islam is the religion of Muslims, who make up more than 90 percent of Afghanistan. There are two Muslim groups, the Sunnis (about 80 percent of Afghans) and the Shi'ite (mostly Hazaras). Muslims believe in one God, Allah. They live according to a sacred book called the Koran, which is filled with the beliefs of Muhammad, the founder of the Islamic religion. Muslims pray five times a day to Allah, often at exquisitely decorated mosques.

THE ROYAL SHAHS

Hamid Karzai is a moderate Muslim who comes from the largest ethnic group, the Pushtuns. The Karzais are from the Popolzai tribe, who can be traced to Afghanistan's first king, Ahmed Shah Durrani, who ruled in the mid-1700s. Durrani was responsible for establishing the city of Kandahar. Most of Afghanistan's leaders, like the Karzais, have come from the Popolzai tribe.

A period of unrest followed Durrani's reign in Afghanistan. Various groups fought for control. The 1800s were met with a series of foreign invasions, during which Persia (now Iran), Great Britain, and Russia all fought for control. By the early 1900s, Great Britain had control of Afghanistan. Then, in 1919, Shah Aman Allah won Afghanistan its independence and moved the country toward modernization.

In 1929, after rebel Habibullah Kalakani held brief control of Afghanistan from January to September, tribal chiefs elected Nadir Shah as the king of Afghanistan. While king, Nadir Shah assembled a Loya Jirga. The Loya Jirga is unique to Afghanistan. It is a traditional gathering—one dating back more than a thousand years—of many of Afghanistan's tribal leaders, representing all ethnic groups. These tribal elders present national issues and try to resolve problems through discussion. The Loya Jirga believes in democracy and everyone's right to respect and fair treatment.

Nadir's Loya Jirga, with 301 tribal elders in attendance, passed a new constitution in 1930. This constitution remained the foundation of the Afghan government for 34 years.

In 1933, King Nadir Shah was assassinated by a young man whose family had been feuding with Nadir since he claimed the throne. Nadir's 19-year-old son, Zahir Shah, became the king. Zahir Shah, who ruled Afghanistan from 1933 to 1973, looked to his uncles for advice in running the country during the early years of his reign. As he got older, Zahir no longer depended on them. For the first 30 years of his rule, Zahir headed an absolute monarchy. In an absolute monarchy, the king or queen has complete political authority; he or she is not obliged to adhere to a constitution, a parliament, or any law. Zahir assembled a Loya Jirga in 1941. The tribal elders voted to keep Afghanistan neutral during World War II (1939–1945), to which Zahir agreed. The decision allowed Afghanistan to make it through World War II nearly unscathed.

Throughout Zahir's rule and during Nadir's earlier reign, the Soviet Union, which then directly bordered Afghanistan, tried to stay politically close to Afghanistan. The Soviet Union was quick to offer financial and military support whenever Afghanistan needed it. In the 1950s, the Soviets helped Afghanistan build schools, roads, and irrigation systems. The Soviets' hope was to turn Afghanistan into a Communist country like itself. Both Nadir and Zahir, however, wanted to distance themselves from the Soviet Union's aid and strengthen Afghanistan to be a more fully independent country.

Mohammad Daoud, Afghanistan's prime minister and a cousin to King Zahir Shah, disagreed with Zahir's philosophy. Daoud worked closely with the Soviet Union and had no problem accepting money to build up the military and buy weapons. He also aimed to modernize Afghanistan. At this time, Afghan women were expected to wear a veil to cover their faces and heads when in public. Daoud pushed for laws to remove the veil from Afghan women. Daoud upheld his beliefs with an iron fist,

Seen here in a May 1965 photograph, Zahir Shah was the absolute ruler of Afghanistan from 1933 to 1973. He possessed complete power over the people and government until he was deposed in a coup and forced into exile in Italy.

though. He had people thrown in jail for opposing his views. He quickly lost the support of the Afghan people.

Daoud tried to create an independent Pushtun nation in 1963, but Zahir removed him from office before he had the chance. In 1964, after convening a 452-member Loya Jirga, Zahir signed a new liberal constitution, which greatly increased women's rights in Afghanistan. Under the constitution, women were granted the right to vote, teach, and work in particular fields, like industry and health care. The new constitution created a parliamentary democracy with a constitutional monarchy. Now, instead of having complete control, Zahir Shah had his political authority limited by the constitution he signed. He wanted the people of Afghanistan to be more involved in their government, and hoped to see an even broader-based government in the years to come.

A POLITICAL TRADITION

Hamid Karzai was born on December 24, 1957, a little more than halfway through Zahir's reign. At the time, his family lived in Kandahar, which had become the second largest city in Afghanistan. Here, Karzai attended his first three years of primary school. Kandahar was a prosperous city that had a good transportation system with an international airport and many roads connecting it to other important cities. Kandahar produced cotton, fresh and dried fruit, and tobacco.

The Karzais were wealthy and lived in a large house. They were considerably better off than most Afghans. In addition to having a lot of money, the Karzais received considerable respect from other Pushtuns. Karzai's father, Abdul Ahad, was a peaceful man. He did not support the use of guns or violence. Hamid and other members of the Pushtun tribe admired him for these views. Abdul Ahad opened his door to all Afghans and listened to their concerns and ideas. Hamid watched his father interact with people of all classes and modeled his own behavior after his father's beliefs and actions.

Hamid was the fifth of eight children. His siblings are Abdul Ahmad, Qayum, Faozia Royan (his only sister), Mahmood, Shah Wali, Ahmad Wali, and Abdul Wali. When not in school, Hamid and his siblings and cousins spent their days playing cricket and baseball. Karzai also enjoyed riding a horse around the courtyard near his home.

Karzai's father and older brothers probably spent much of their time in the local teahouses. Found throughout Afghanistan, the teahouses provided a setting in which people could gather to discuss politics or catch up on family news. When Karzai was in college, he, too, spent afternoons in teahouses, discussing culture and politics with his professors and fellow students.

The Karzais come from a long line of political figures. They are even distantly related to the royal Shah family; both are from the same clan. Over the years, the Karzai and Shah families had intermarried. Karzai's grandfather, Khair Mohamed Karzai, was the deputy minister of the interior. He worked in the Afghan senate that authorized King Zahir Shah to rule. Karzai's father worked for Zahir as a senator in the Afghan parliament during the end of his reign. When the Soviets tried to take over Afghanistan, Karzai's father worked to strengthen the Afghan resistance movement. All of the southern Pushtun tribes greatly respected Abdul Ahad Karzai for his wisdom and intelligence. The Popolzai tribe made Abdul Ahad its chief, an honor he kept until he died in 1999.

Abdul Ahad Karzai moved his family to Kabul, Afghanistan's capital and the largest city, when he became speaker of the parliament. Beautiful mosques can be found throughout the city, which has both old and new sections. In the old section the Karzais could shop at the local bazaars. At these outdoor marketplaces, people could buy everything from food to clothing to housewares. The city's new section had a university and a museum. The weather in Kabul is similar to that in Denver, Colorado. In the winter, heavy snows fall, sometimes shutting the city down for days at a time. In the summer, it is hot and dry with little rainfall.

In Kabul, Karzai continued his education. After elementary school, he attended Habibia High School, which had originally opened in 1903 and was the first modern school in Kabul. Karzai was a quiet, serious student. He dreamed of going to the

As a young man, Karzai lived with his family in the city of Kabul, a major population and cultural center of Afghanistan both then and now. In Kabul, visitors could experience extraordinary architecture as well as bustling trade, like the shopping being done at this outdoor market in the city.

University of Kabul, which was well respected at the time. Karzai thought he might follow in his father's footsteps and work in the parliament.

When he was not in school, Karzai knew how to have fun. He took in movies and listened to good music—luxuries to which the average Afghan did not have access. Karzai also loved to read. He studied Darwin and learned about the evolution of humans. He read Charles Dickens and Anton Chekhov. He learned about Henry Kissinger and the Reverend Dr. Martin Luther King, Jr. Karzai continually found joy in learning.

3

Soviet Invasion

Mohammad Daoud overthrew his cousin, King Zahir Shah, in 1973. Daoud waited until Zahir Shah was out of town and then took over the government in a bloodless coup. Daoud forced Zahir Shah into exile in Rome, Italy, where he remained for more than 20 years. Hamid Karzai and his family remained closely allied to Zahir during his years in exile. Like Zahir, the Karzais hoped for a broad-based government for Afghanistan.

When Daoud put an end to Zahir's monarchy, he declared Afghanistan a republic. From the time Daoud had begun to work in his cousin's monarchy in the 1950s and 1960s, Daoud had maintained tight relations with the Soviet Union. In fact, due in large part to Daoud's close communications with them, the Soviets had trained nearly 90 percent of the Afghan army, and many Afghans traveled to the Soviet Union to go to college. Eventually, though, Daoud became

During the early and mid-1970s, after King Zahir Shah was overthrown, Afghanistan had a close friendship with the Soviet Union, which provided military training for the Afghan army and education for civilians. Seen here in a 1959 photograph is Afghan leader Sardar Mohammed Daoud (right), who led the country after Zahir Shah's ousting, shaking hands with Soviet Premier Nikita Khrushchev.

worried that Afghanistan was too dependent on the Soviets and he started to get rid of Communist officials who held positions in the Afghan government.

SCHOOL DAYS

In 1976, Karzai left Afghanistan and traveled to India, which is east of Pakistan. He first attended a local college in Shimla, India, and then was admitted to Himachal Pradesh University in the same city. He boarded at the YMCA, grew his hair long, and wore bell-bottom pants. Karzai walked every-where—to his classes, to local teahouses, and through Shimla's thick forests—which he feels helped keep him fit and healthy.

Karzai studied political science and international relations at Himachal Pradesh. He enjoyed college, as he had primary school and high school, and did very well. He was well liked by his teachers and spent many hours talking with them about Afghanistan's history, culture, and politics. One former teacher remembers Karzai being "polished and broadminded." Karzai graduated with a master's degree in 1982, six years after arriving in Shimla.

During his college years, Karzai became a huge fan of Mohandas Gandhi's writings. Karzai read many of Gandhi's works. Karzai liked Gandhi's nonviolent ways of working through problems, and like Gandhi, believed that guns and violence were not the answer to overcoming conflicts. Gandhi's beliefs mirrored those of Karzai's father, as well as Karzai's own.

Karzai also learned to speak English during his days in Shimla. When he first arrived in the city, he lived with a local family. The family's two daughters taught Karzai to speak, read, and write English. He had now mastered six languages: Pushtu (the language most Pushtuns speak), Dari (the language most Tajiks and some urban Pushtuns speak), Urdu (the language spoken by Hindu merchants), French, Hindi, and English.

PEOPLE'S DEMOCRATIC PARTY OF AFGHANISTAN

Meanwhile, the People's Democratic Party of Afghanistan (PDPA), a Communist organization, was gaining power in Afghanistan. The PDPA was divided into two factions: Nur Mohammad Taraki led the Khalq faction and Babrak Karmal led the Parcham faction. Both were Communists and used the Soviet Union as a model for their politics, but the two factions did not get along. The Khalq was larger and more radical than the Parcham. In 1978, the Parcham repeatedly tried to overthrow the Khalq, but was unsuccessful.

Despite factional fighting, the Khalq and Parcham factions united long enough to overthrow Daoud and establish a

Communist government in Afghanistan. In April 1978, the PDPA killed Daoud during the Saur (April) Revolution. The PDPA took control of Afghanistan and proclaimed it the Democratic Republic of Afghanistan. Nur Mohammad Taraki became its prime minister, Babrak Karmal its deputy prime minister, and Hafizullah Amin its foreign minister.

During this time, Afghan Communists and Soviets killed or imprisoned many Afghan tribal elders and leaders. Hamid's father, Abdul Ahad Karzai, was put in prison. Other family members were also imprisoned or killed. Abdul Ahad, along with many other Afghans, was eventually set free. Released in 1981, after two years in prison, Abdul Ahad began to fight the Soviets with all he had.

Afghan opposition to the Communist government quickly spread. Soon after its takeover, the PDPA and its army were engaged in warfare all over Afghanistan. The PDPA turned to the Soviets for help.

An extreme rivalry also existed between Amin and Taraki, who were both members of the Khalq faction and who both wanted control of it. In September 1979, an unknown assassin killed Taraki, and Amin quickly seized power, hoping to govern Afghanistan as an independent ruler. Amin was known as a ruthless leader. If someone disagreed with him, that person was killed. During Amin's two-month leadership, tens of thousands of Afghans died.

The Soviets were wary of Amin; they suspected that he had killed Taraki, who had been more supportive of the Soviet Union. The Soviets soon realized that Amin was going to try to rule Afghanistan independently, without their backing. The Soviets marched into Afghanistan with their powerful Red army on December 24, 1979. Just two days later, they had secured Kabul. They quickly killed Amin and named Babrak Karmal president of Afghanistan. During the ensuing ten-year occupation, the number of Soviet troops in Afghanistan grew from about 30,000 to more than 100,000.

AFGHANISTAN'S REACTION TO SOVIET OCCUPATION

Communism was taking over Afghanistan, and a large number of Afghan college students had joined the Communist fight. Until this time, Afghanistan had been ruled mostly by kings, but across the country, individual warlords owned large sections of land. They protected their land and territories, their families, their ethnic beliefs, and their religion by forming private militias. The warlords fought among themselves and tried to gain land and power through force. They were often independently wealthy and considered themselves above the law.

There was also a small middle-class group in Afghanistan. These people owned a small amount of land and were able to grow just enough food to feed their families. The majority of Afghans, however, were sharecroppers, who worked the large tracts of land that the warlords owned. These people had barely enough money to survive and were forced to depend heavily on the warlords.

Some young college-age males wanted this hierarchy to stop. They wanted to see the wealth spread across the country—not just in the hands of a few. They saw communism as a way to end warlordism and bring unity to Afghanistan. To these young men, communism was a welcome change.

Other Afghans, like Hamid Karzai, did not become Communists. Although they did want to see warlordism end, they did not agree with communism. They wanted to see an independent Afghanistan with a broad-based government— one that represents a wide range of Afghan groups. Karzai, and others like him, left the country rather than continue their education in Afghanistan. With the best colleges in the country located in Soviet-occupied Kabul, the young Afghans had little choice but to leave.

LIVING IN EXILE

After Karzai finished his studies in India in 1982, he rejoined his father and the rest of the family in Quetta,

Pakistan, where they had moved in 1981 to escape the Communist government of Afghanistan. The Karzais hoped to return one day to their homeland, so they always made a point of renting, not buying, their homes in Pakistan.

The Karzais were not the only Afghans to leave the country during the Soviet occupation. Many Afghans opposed the occupation, and as a result, more than 5 million of them became refugees in neighboring Pakistan and Iran. Another 2 million became displaced in their homeland.

Some Afghan refugees, including most of Karzai's brothers and his sister, moved to the United States. Six of Karzai's siblings moved there to attend college after they finished high school. Five of these six opened a chain of successful Afghan restaurants called Helmand, after the river near where the Karzais grew up in Kandahar. The Karzais have restaurants in Maryland, Massachusetts, and California. Karzai's youngest brother, Abdul Wali, is an assistant professor of biochemistry at the State University of New York at Stony Brook and conducts medical research on antibiotics. He lives on Long Island with his wife and daughter. Hamid Karzai stays in touch with all his siblings, and they visit each other as often as they can.

While in exile, Karzai wanted to help end the foreign occupation of his country. He joined the Afghan Jihad wing of the Afghan National Liberation Front (ANLF), based in Peshawar, Pakistan. The people in this organization, led by Sibghatullah Mojadidi, hoped to see the Soviet invaders thrown out of Afghanistan. In 1982, Karzai became the director of operations of the ANLF. People respected Karzai's ability to listen as well as speak.

During the early 1980s, Karzai and other ANLF members supported a newly formed Afghan resistance movement of fighters called the mujahideen. People in the West called them "freedom fighters." The mujahideen fought to push the Soviets out of Afghanistan. Karzai worked to help them; he talked to leaders around the world, including some in the United States, to persuade

After the Soviet occupation, many Afghans struggled to find a way to retake control of their country. Hamid Karzai was one of many politically active people who supported the training of "mujahideen," or freedom fighters, to oppose the Soviet forces.

them to send weapons, ammunition, and financial aid to support the Afghan resistance movement. Gradually, the mujahideen grew stronger and became a force to be reckoned with.

SOVIET OCCUPATION

Although the Soviets had more soldiers, the mujahideen were able to contain the Soviets' control to the capital city of Kabul. Several factors contributed to this. The mujahideen were getting a steady supply of aid from Pakistan and the United States. The mujahideen also knew the Afghan countryside much better than the Soviets did. Only a few roads ran out of Kabul, so the mujahideen could fairly easily concentrate on ambushing any Soviets who tried to travel on them. The only way the Soviets could leave Kabul was with the protection of heavily armored tanks.

Meanwhile, from Pakistan, Karzai was working as a mujahideen advisor and diplomat. He continued to work with countries around the world to get the financial aid and weapons that the mujahideen needed. During this time, Karzai established strong relations with the United States, which considered Karzai an ally.

Changes developed in the Soviet Union in 1985 when a new leader, Mikhail Gorbachev, took power. Gorbachev was not interested in continuing the Soviet occupation of Afghanistan. Keeping the Red army in Afghanistan cost a lot of money, hurting the Soviet economy. In addition, other Muslim countries had begun to distance themselves from the Soviet Union—a development that Gorbachev did not like to see. In 1987, the Soviets replaced Karmal, Afghanistan's president, with Communist Sayid Mohammed Najibullah while they tried to figure out how to withdraw the Red army. Karmal left Afghanistan to live in Moscow.

Then, in April 1988, representatives from Afghanistan, the Soviet Union, Pakistan, and the United States met in Geneva, Switzerland, to resolve the conflict between Afghanistan and the Soviet Union. The result was a cease-fire and an agreement for Soviet troops to withdraw. Troops began to leave Afghanistan in May 1988. The remaining troops withdrew by February 1989. The Soviet occupation was over.

During the ten-year Soviet occupation of Kabul, the city itself received very little damage. None of the schools, mosques, or museums there was hurt during the fighting. Much of the fighting had taken place in rural areas outside of Kabul. Although the capital city was not badly damaged, the number of Afghan lives lost during the Soviet occupation was enormous. About one million Afghans were killed. Some 15,000 Soviet soldiers died, and 37,000 Soviet soldiers were wounded.

The killing did not stop after the Soviets pulled out. The Soviets had planted millions of mines across Afghanistan. Most were unmarked. Some were disguised as children's toys.

Despite their lengthy stay in Afghanistan, Soviet troops were never able to subdue the nation entirely. By February 1989, when this photograph of departing Soviet soldiers was taken, all the occupying troops had withdrawn.

Children would pick up what they thought was a toy, and an explosive would be set off, killing everyone within a certain area. Although the United Nations (UN) oversaw mine-removal operations, the deadly mines continued to cause harm long after the Soviets left Afghanistan.

THE MUJAHIDEEN

President Najibullah remained in control of Afghanistan until 1992—although, in reality, the mujahideen ruled the Afghan countryside. Then, in April 1992, the mujahideen overthrew Najibullah. Now that the mujahideen had rid the country of communism, many leaders, such as Karzai, hoped that Afghanistan would finally have peace and unity. They did not get their wish.

Mujahideen rule was, in many ways, similar to the Communists' rule. Like the Communists, the mujahideen could not agree on who should lead the country, and there was

much fighting among mujahideen members. Three factions—
the Tajiks, the Uzbeks, and the Hazaras—had combined to form
one large coalition called the Northern Alliance, led by
Burhanuddin Rabbani. They wanted to run the Afghan government without the numerous Pushtun factions, the largest of
which was led by Gulbuddin Hekmatyar. Hekmatyar, in turn,
began attacking Kabul with powerful missiles, causing great
destruction in the city. These factions continued to fight for years.

Karzai returned to Afghanistan in 1992 to serve as a deputy
foreign minister under the mujahideen government. During
the Soviet occupation, Karzai had gained great respect from
members of the mujahideen. They hoped that Karzai could
continue to get the foreign support and backing they needed to
keep the mujahideen government strong.

As deputy foreign minister, Karzai frequently visited the
United States to discuss Afghanistan's politics with officials
there. During his visits, Karzai often stayed with his brother
Qayum and Qayum's wife, Pat, in their home in Maryland. Just
as he had done in college, Karzai enjoyed taking long walks—
this time through the Maryland countryside.

In 1992, Rabbani, the Northern Alliance leader, became
president of an interim government that lasted until 1996. Still,
factional fighting continued. Within each faction, warlords led
their privately owned militias to try to overthrow the government, gain more land, or settle political disputes. In just a few
years after Rabbani took office, some 50,000 Afghans were
killed. Kabul was the site of much fighting, and much of the
city now lay in ruins. Some schools had to be shut down
because of structural damage. Children were left without an
opportunity for an education. Streets were not safe to walk on
because of continued shooting. Karzai was fed up with the
fighting. He resigned from his post as deputy foreign minister
in 1994 and returned to Pakistan. Anarchy had taken over
much of Afghanistan.

4

The Rise of
the Taliban

A new Islamic movement, led by Mullah Mohammad Omar, first appeared in Kandahar in 1994. Members of the movement were called the Taliban. *Taliban* is a Persian word meaning "student." The Taliban promised the people of Afghanistan order and stability, two things Afghans longed for. As a result, many Afghans joined the Taliban, including Hamid Karzai, who wanted to see strength and consistency in his country.

In hopes of seeing the Taliban succeed in its promises of order and stability, Karzai gave the Taliban $50,000. Karzai met with Omar on several occasions and also gave the Taliban a huge supply of weapons, which he had acquired over the years and stored away. Karzai would later come to regret this generosity.

Another Islamic group, Al Qaeda, or the International Islamic Front, had formed five years earlier, in 1989. Al Qaeda's focus on Islam

When the Taliban began to fight for control of the Afghan government in 1994, many Afghans, including Karzai, supported them because they promised to bring peace and order to the nation, which had spent years of turmoil under Soviet occupation. Here, Taliban militia soldiers are seen praying for victory before a battle against government forces in October 1996.

is similar to the Taliban's, but Al Qaeda is far more radical in its operations and scope. Al Qaeda is an international terrorist group whose purpose is to use force and violence to oppose non-Islamic governments, like that of the United States. The leader of Al Qaeda, Osama bin Laden, came to know Mullah Mohammad Omar around the year 2000. Omar used bin Laden's highly skilled fighters in some of his battles with Afghan warlords, and bin Laden recruited the most dedicated students from Omar's religious schools to join his terrorist missions.

WHO WERE THE TALIBAN?

Mullah Mohammad Omar, like Karzai, had grown up in Afghanistan in Kandahar. But while Karzai was well off and educated, Omar was poor and received little education as a child. While Karzai grew up to travel all around the world, though, Omar is said to have left Kandahar only a few times in his life. In fact, most Taliban leaders had very little education and had grown up in small Afghan villages.

Omar wanted to make Afghanistan the purest Islamic state in the world. He envisioned a male-dominated society in which the people spent their time praying and living the life he thought God intended. His views became the basis for the Taliban's beliefs.

The Taliban included several different groups of people. There were young, homeless Afghan boys trying to make it in refugee camps in Pakistan; there were college-age Afghan men living in Pakistani refugee camps; and there were former mujahideen. They all sought unity and a place to belong, which they found in Taliban-run religious schools, called madrasas, set up in Pakistani cities like Peshawar and Quetta. Later, madrasas were also set up in Afghanistan. At these schools, Taliban members taught students to live by Islamic law. The schools doubled as military training camps. Students practiced shooting and learned how to use a variety of weapons.

The young homeless Afghan boys' parents were either away fighting wars in Afghanistan or too poor to continue taking care of their children. Sending their male children to the Taliban-run religious schools was a way of ensuring that they would have a roof over their heads and food in their stomachs. The boys coming from these situations often had no education at all. They were impressionable and eager to feel like they belonged to something.

The college-age Afghan men and the mujahideen had grown up with guns and violence their entire lives. They had watched the Soviets invade their country. They had seen warlords and the mujahideen fight over control of land. They had witnessed countless killings and unfair treatment. These men wanted something more for their country—unity. They thought the Taliban could make that happen. They wanted to be part of a growing movement that appeared to be finally putting an end to the constant fighting.

TAKING CONTROL OF AFGHANISTAN

After taking over Kandahar in 1994, the Taliban fought local warlords and began to gain more territory in Afghanistan. In November 1994, after learning about the newly organized Taliban and their successful fighting, Pakistan hired the Taliban to protect a convoy delivering goods from Pakistan to Central Asia. After this successful appointment, Pakistan fully supported the Taliban and the Pakistani intelligence service offered the Taliban military assistance.

The Taliban became known as people fed up with post-Soviet Afghanistan, and they quickly gained further support. Many Pushtuns joined in hopes of reclaiming power from the Northern Alliance.

In November 1994, the Taliban successfully captured Lashkar-gah. On September 11, 1996, they took control of the eastern city of Jalalabad, which borders Pakistan. On September 27 of the same year, the Taliban gained control of Kabul. When they took over the capital, they forced out President Rabbani, who went on to join forces with the Northern Alliance to fight the Taliban. Most countries still considered Rabbani the head of Afghanistan, even though the Taliban had taken control of Kabul. By June 1997, the Taliban had control of two-thirds of Afghanistan.

Once the Taliban controlled the majority of Afghanistan, they began to lay out strict rules for Afghans to follow. The list of what Afghans could not do grew daily. The two things the Taliban did allow were for people to pray to God and to serve Afghanistan. They banned all television, movies, computer and

Under the oppressive Taliban regime, women were allowed no rights at all. In fact, they were not even permitted to be seen in public unless they were wearing a burqa like this woman's—a head-to-toe garment that completely covered the body and also made it difficult for the woman to see her surroundings clearly.

Internet use, and music. They banned children's toys, cameras, paintings of people and animals, cigarettes and alcohol, magazines and newspapers, pool tables, and firecrackers. Children could not fly kites. Men were not allowed to cut or trim their beards. The Taliban made it illegal for women to go to school or work, to ride bicycles, show their ankles, wear makeup or high-heeled shoes, and even to laugh in public. Women were expected to stay indoors unless accompanied by a male relative. The Taliban justified the harshness of their treatment of women by saying it was part of Islamic law.

The Rise of the Taliban 37

CHANGING SIDES

Karzai and other Afghans quickly became suspicious of the Taliban movement. A moderate Muslim, Karzai did not agree with the lengthy list of illegal activities. More and more Pakistani and Arab extremists, like Osama bin Laden, associated with the Taliban movement. Gradually, these extremists dominated the movement and became its leaders.

The Taliban were ruthless and powerful. Many of their leaders had much money and many guns. They killed thousands of Afghans who tried to oppose them. With bombs and gunfire, they destroyed large numbers of homes as well as the country-side. The Taliban's rules were mandatory. People who defied them were tortured, jailed, or even killed. For example, if a woman wore nailpolish in public, she might have a finger cut off. If a man trimmed or cut his beard, he would be imprisoned until the beard grew full and bushy again.

When Mullah Mohammad Omar asked Karzai to be the Taliban's UN ambassador in 1995, Karzai refused. One year later, Karzai once again left the country to live in exile in Pakistan. There, he and his father worked together to campaign against the Taliban.

For the next few years, Karzai spent a great deal of his time traveling around the world to speak to government officials about the destruction happening in Afghanistan. Unfortunately, the leaders did not take his claims very seriously. Karzai tried to convince them that the extremists who had taken over the Taliban were capable of horrible terrorist acts. He had seen firsthand the Taliban's ruthless killing. Anyone who did not follow the Taliban's laws or did not agree with their methods risked death. Killing had become common across Afghanistan.

Karzai was rarely at home anymore. He spent days, even weeks, abroad, spreading the word about who the Taliban were and what they had the power to do. The Taliban had large amounts of money, power, and weaponry, and Karzai wanted to equip the people of Afghanistan with the same forces so they could defend themselves against the Taliban. Although international government officials did not take action, Karzai did not stop talking. He planned to keep on spreading the word until he finally received the support he needed to help stop the Taliban.

A few other leaders were trying to stop the Taliban as well. King Zahir Shah, still living in exile in Rome, tried to organize a Loya Jirga to choose a new Afghan government, but the Taliban refused to comply with his request. Karzai would later take up Zahir's attempts at organizing a Loya Jirga.

MARRIAGE

Until this point in Karzai's life, he had devoted all his time and energy to politics. He was now 40 years old and still single. Most Afghan men marry in their early twenties. Afghans do not usually choose their spouses; marriages are arranged by parents. It is very common for parents to choose a cousin as a spouse for their child. If they choose a spouse outside the family, the groom's family must pay a bride-price to the bride's family.

Karzai did not view marriage as a high priority. He wanted only to focus on creating a better Afghanistan. His life revolved around politics, so he had not spent time or energy thinking about marriage or family. When Karzai's mother became ill around this time, she told Karzai that she would like to see him married before she died. Karzai decided to oblige.

In January 1999, Karzai married his cousin, Zinat, in a marriage arranged by Karzai's parents. Hamid and Zinat live in a modest, two-story house in Kabul. At present, they do not have any children. Zinat Karzai was once a doctor, specializing in gynecology, but she no longer maintains her practice. As a doctor, she had worked to help the Afghan refugees in Pakistan. Now she remains mostly at home, surrounded by guards and special security, due in part to the family's fear of her being kidnapped.

Zinat grew up in Kandahar, where she attended high school. She moved to Kabul to attend the University of Kabul.

Although Karzai (seen here) was generally more interested in politics and building his own career than in family and romance, he married his cousin, Zinat, in January 1999.

When the factional fighting began in Kabul in 1992, Zinat and her family moved to Quetta, Pakistan.

Many Afghans, especially women, would like to see more of Zinat. She has never made a public appearance with Hamid Karzai; therefore, reporters have never photographed the couple together. In Afghan culture, it is considered a disgrace if a man in a high position shows his wife in public. The few times Zinat has agreed to interviews have been with the certainty there would be no cameras or microphones. She has only given interviews to female interviewers.

TRAGEDY IN THE KARZAI FAMILY

On July 14, 1999, just six months after Karzai married Zinat, Hamid's 75-year-old father, Abdul Ahad, was shot and killed in Quetta, Pakistan. Abdul Ahad had just spent his evening praying at a local mosque. When he finished, he left the mosque with two other gentlemen. They gathered near the entrance gate to talk briefly. The killer shot at the men; Abdul Ahad was shot in the back.

Abdul Ahad was rushed to the hospital, but died shortly after arrival. That which he had hated all his life—guns—turned out to be what took his life in the end. Karzai later told reporters he was glad that his father had not seen the gunman, since his father would not have wanted to see a gun pointed at him. The other two men, who had accompanied Abdul Ahad to the mosque, also died. The killer was never found but is believed to have been a member of the Taliban. Many Afghans believe the Taliban feared the Karzais because they were well-educated and prominent political figures. Most likely, feeling threatened by Abdul Ahad's anti-Taliban activities and influence, the Taliban had the leader of the Popolzai tribe killed.

Hamid and his family transported Abdul Ahad's body in a 300-vehicle procession to the family's burial ground in Karz, near Kandahar, which was also the Taliban stronghold. Parading through this stronghold was an act of defiance against the Taliban, but one that the Taliban did not try to stop. They knew that hundreds of thousands of Afghans had respected Abdul Ahad Karzai. Hamid Karzai's determination to bury his father in Karz showed the Taliban and the world that Karzai was a prominent leader of resistance to the Taliban. Thousands of people gathered the next day to pay their respects to a much-admired leader.

Karzai was deeply saddened by his father's death. He also became more determined than ever to bring peace to Afghanistan and stop the Taliban. He used the tragic event as fuel to continue his plans to bring down the Taliban.

On July 22, 1999, Afghan leaders and Islamic scholars named Hamid Karzai as the new leader of the Popolzai tribe. Like his father, he had long supported former King Zahir Shah's plan for a broad-based government in Afghanistan. He also hoped to bring back the Loya Jirga. Karzai met with Zahir in Italy. The two allies spoke about Karzai's new position as leader of the Popolzais and his hope of establishing a broad-based government. Zahir gave him a copy of the holy Koran in a heartfelt gesture of friendship. Karzai soon became known as the "King of Kandahar."

5

The Fall of the Taliban

Afghanistan was in a state of fear and unrest in late 1999 and 2000. It had no official form of government. The Taliban and Al Qaeda continued to train Afghan and Pakistani men to kill and terrorize. The country was purely militarized; nearly every person had a weapon. Children were not being educated, women were forced to stay at home, and men and boys were on the streets killing.

Controlling more than 90 percent of Afghanistan in 2000, the Taliban wanted global recognition. They wanted to be the official leaders of Afghanistan and hold a seat at the United Nations. At this time, only three countries recognized the Taliban as the government of Afghanistan: Pakistan, Saudi Arabia, and the United Arab Emirates. Most countries still considered President Burhanuddin Rabbani the leader of Afghanistan, even though the Taliban had forced him out of Kabul in 1996. Rabbani continued to hold the Afghan seat at the United Nations.

In March 2001, the Taliban destroyed two nearly 2,000-year-old Buddha statues in the city of Bamiyan in central Afghanistan. The ancient sandstone statues had been carved into a cliff during the third century. One statue was 175 feet (53.3 meters) high, and the other stood at 120 feet (36.6 meters). Taliban officials ordered the statues to be destroyed because they were considered un-Islamic representations of the human form. The Taliban used rockets and mortars to destroy the ancient works of art.

Afghans were outraged by the Taliban's actions. They wanted to act against them, but feared what the Taliban might then do. The largest and strongest concentration of the Taliban, headed by Mullah Mohammad Omar, was near Karzai's birth town, Kandahar. It was essential to Afghanistan and its people to reclaim Kandahar and regain their country.

Karzai was trying to do just that. Clearly, the Taliban did not like the Karzais, especially Hamid, who openly continued his anti-Taliban activities. In Afghanistan, he took daily three-hour walks around cities to talk to the people and assess the effects of the Taliban. He took few precautions for his own safety. He felt that what was most important was to keep in touch with the Afghan people and know what was happening in Afghanistan.

Karzai also maintained close relations with the United States and other countries, reporting his findings on what was happening in his country. Karzai continued to travel to the United States, meeting with members of the Central Intelligence Agency (CIA) and other government officials to discuss the Taliban and the threat of terrorist attacks.

Karzai was a well-respected diplomat and speaker. He now had much experience traveling around the globe to talk to world leaders. He knew how to present issues so that people would listen. For example, Karzai visited Tokyo, Japan, after the Taliban had destroyed the Buddha statues. Before going, he

Despite the disapproval of most Afghans, the Taliban used powerful weapons to destroy ancient statues of Buddha in March 2001. These men are standing in front of the ruins of what was once the tallest standing statue of Buddha in Bamiyan City in central Afghanistan.

learned a bit of Japanese to include in his speeches. Talking to the Japanese, he also described how the Taliban's destruction of the Buddha statues made him feel personally. His ability to personalize his speeches and draw in his audience helped make him a good politician.

In addition to his travels, Karzai began to think about assembling his own militia to work against the Taliban. Although he believed in nonviolence, he felt the only way to stop the Taliban, itself such an incredibly violent organization, was with force. Karzai also wanted to gain support of tribal leaders who could help to lobby for an assembly of the Loya Jirga. Through a Loya Jirga, Afghans could choose a new government.

TERRORISM IN THE UNITED STATES

In 2001, what Karzai had been talking about for years with foreign officials—his worries about terrorism and the capabilities of the Taliban—became all too real. On September 11, 2001, disaster struck the United States. Osama bin Laden, head of the Al Qaeda organization, ordered terrorist attacks on the United States.

Bin Laden targeted the United States for several reasons: first, because the United States has a non-Islamic government; second, because the United States maintains close ties with Israel, which occupies land that many Muslims consider rightfully theirs; and third, because the United States keeps military bases in Saudi Arabia and Kuwait, both Muslim countries. People in Al Qaeda believe that the United States is stealing oil from Saudi Arabia and Kuwait.

The Al Qaeda terrorists hijacked four commercial U.S. airplanes. The first plane crashed into the north tower of the World Trade Center in New York City at 8:46 A.M. Sixteen minutes later, a second plane hit the south tower. The planes hit near the top of each tower. After the first plane hit, thousands of people from both buildings began to evacuate. Some people on the top floors jumped from windows to their deaths. Both

The United States was changed forever by the tragic events of September 11, 2001. After Muslim extremists crashed commercial airplanes into the twin towers of the World Trade Center and the Pentagon, people around the world demanded the removal of the Taliban government in Afghanistan, which had long supported violent terrorists, including those responsible for the events of September 11.

towers completely crumbled and fell to the ground within a couple of hours of the initial crashes. Some surrounding buildings caved in as well. A third plane flew into the Pentagon near Washington, D.C. The fourth plane, which was probably also headed for Washington, D.C., crashed in a Pennsylvania field after some of the passengers tried to stop the hijackers. All of the people aboard died instantly.

More than 3,000 people died on that tragic day. Husbands and wives lost spouses, and children lost parents. Hundreds of banks, financial corporations, and other businesses housed in the towers lost employees and databases. For 99 days after the attack on the World Trade Center, fires continued to burn in New York City. Firefighters, police officers, and volunteers eventually removed 1.8 billion tons of debris from the site. The cost to clean up the ruins was around $600 million.

Osama bin Laden was found to be directly responsible for the attacks. Since the horrific act of terrorism, bin Laden has not been found. The Taliban was held responsible for hiding bin Laden, since they refused to take action against him, claiming he was a guest in their country.

After September 11, Afghanistan suddenly gained world-wide attention. The United States wanted desperately to find Osama bin Laden and bring down the Taliban. Afghanistan had spent years fighting the Taliban alone; now other countries, particularly the United States, wanted to fight them as well.

RETURNING TO AFGHANISTAN

As a result of the September 11 attacks, the Taliban lost the backing of two of its three supporters: Pakistan and the United Arab Emirates. Although Pakistani President Pervez Musharraf had fully backed the Taliban for years, he sided with the United States after the attacks. Countries around the world wanted to put an end to the Taliban and Al Qaeda. In Afghanistan, the Northern Alliance still controlled the rugged mountains in the northeast—the only area not inhabited by the Taliban—and it worked to regain land from the Taliban by heading south.

In early October 2001, Karzai decided it was time to leave Quetta, Pakistan, and return to Afghanistan to fight the Taliban himself. The day before Karzai entered Afghanistan, U.S. President George W. Bush ordered air strikes on Afghanistan to try to eliminate the Taliban and Al Qaeda. The forces sought out Taliban compounds, where they thought bin Laden might be hiding. The U.S. military effort became known as Operation Enduring Freedom.

Karzai did not talk to many people about his plans to sneak into Afghanistan. He knew it would be a dangerous mission. The border between Pakistan and Afghanistan was heavily protected by Taliban forces. The Taliban did not want Karzai entering Afghanistan. If Karzai were detected, he would most certainly be shot. He waited until the evening he was leaving to tell his wife. Zinat asked him if he would be safe. He responded, "It's something I don't know."

Karzai sneaked into Afghanistan with the help of three men. They rode motorbikes down the main highway and wore turbans to disguise themselves. They carried few weapons and had little ammunition—Karzai himself had neither. At one point, they even had to deal with a flat tire. The four men traveled to Karz, near Karzai's hometown of Kandahar. After reaching the city safely, Karzai continued on to the mountains of Oruzgan Province.

It was not until Karzai was actually in Afghanistan that he realized just how large and strong a force he was up against. He had been under the impression that, although his mission would be dangerous, he could move in and fight off the Taliban without much effort. Karzai was surprised to find out just how well trained and well equipped the Taliban were. Karzai had yet another huge challenge to overcome.

Karzai had spent the last five years organizing anti-Taliban activity, so putting together a force to oppose the Taliban was not difficult. Much of the groundwork was already in place. What he needed to do was spread the word that he was in Afghanistan and ready to fight. In Oruzgan Province, Karzai met with many tribal elders, urging them to join him against the Taliban. Karzai would meet a friend and tell him he wanted to have dinner that night and to invite three or four other tribal elders or chiefs. That evening, Karzai would talk to the elders about the need to bring down the Taliban. The

In the days and weeks after September 11, Karzai actively tried to gain support for the overthrow of the Taliban and for the institution of a new Afghan government. Among other tactics, Karzai (right) held long talks with tribal leaders like those seen here to hear their opinions and to encourage them to help him.

elders would return to their villages and urge villagers to join Karzai's militia.

Gradually, Karzai's presence in Afghanistan became known to the Taliban. Four hundred Taliban troops were on his trail. Karzai and 50 followers headed deep into the mountains, away from villages where innocent Afghans might be killed. Over the next few days, Karzai's group grew to 150 people. However, they had few weapons and no money. The people got together to discuss their options. Then they came to Karzai and asked him to call the United States to supply weapons. Karzai agreed.

He called the United States, and the Americans agreed to send food, ammunition, and weapons, but they needed a location to send the supplies. Karzai and his people were in the middle of the isolated mountains of Afghanistan. They were finally able to give the United States a sketchy location of their whereabouts. The United States told Karzai to light four fires on a particular night. This helped the United States spot them from the air. That night, the United States dropped the goods from airplanes. The very next day, the Taliban forces descended upon Karzai and his people.

With the newly acquired weapons, Karzai and his troops did what they could to defend themselves. Karzai and his people had no real way of knowing whether they had won or lost the battle, as the communications systems in the mountains were undependable. Afraid they had lost, they began to scatter. But Karzai and his group had, in fact, won.

BRINGING DOWN THE TALIBAN

On November 13, 2001, the Northern Alliance stormed Kabul and reclaimed it from the Taliban. The city rejoiced. Citizens blared music in the streets and threw flowers in front of tanks. Through the help of the U.S. army and the Northern Alliance, Afghans had reclaimed much of the territory the Taliban had taken over the last few years. Taliban members started leaving the country or joining the militias of local warlords. The Taliban still hung on to their original stronghold, Kandahar, though.

Karzai's militia force, which came to number 4,000, hoped to bring down the last remaining Taliban forces in Kandahar. Americans, fearing more terrorist attacks, also wanted to stop the Taliban. The United States offered to supply Karzai with armed security to protect him and his militia. Karzai turned down the offer at first, worried that Afghans would not want the continued backing of the United States. As word got out that the Americans were offering well-trained and well-equipped military personnel, though, tribal elders and chiefs encouraged Karzai to accept. They knew they could not defeat the Taliban alone with the weapons they had and wanted the aid of American bombs and the strength of the American army.

The U.S. army's 5th Special Forces Group arrived in Afghanistan to protect Karzai and his growing militia. The Americans continued to drop parachutes with food, supplies, and weapons when needed. The special forces group was able to advance within 20 miles (32 kilometers) of Kandahar by calling in air strikes and stopping Taliban attacks.

Finally, the Taliban leader Mullah Mohammad Omar agreed to surrender Kandahar. Karzai's militia of 4,000 soldiers and the special forces unit put enough pressure on the Taliban that they began to realize they would never gain control of all of Afghanistan.

On December 5, 2001, Hamid Karzai was at the Shawali Kowt district headquarters near Kandahar. Karzai planned to meet with some Taliban leaders later that day to talk about their pending surrender. All of a sudden, there was a huge explosion and Karzai was on the floor—broken doors and windows had flown around and a fine dust now covered the entire room. People near Karzai had thrown their bodies on top of him to protect him from the blast. When Karzai got up, he found injured people all around him. Karzai's face was bleeding from some cuts. At the time, the people at the district headquarters thought the entire town was under siege from attacks. A few hours later, though, they learned that it had been a bomb set off accidentally by the United States. The mistake cost the lives of three U.S. soldiers and at least 23 Afghan fighters. Dozens more were wounded. Later that day, Karzai did meet with the remaining Taliban officials, who delivered their surrender.

Karzai and the United States had managed to put an end to

Assisted by an intensive U.S.-led bombing campaign, Karzai was able to oust the Taliban from control of Afghanistan and become his nation's temporary leader. Here, U.S. forces patrol the streets of Kandahar, Afghanistan, in December 2001, shortly after Karzai's arrival in the city.

the Taliban movement. A former Taliban ambassador told reporters, "We have accepted a deal for peaceful surrender, which will protect the lives and dignity of the Taliban fighters and their leaders. Heavy United States bombing contributed to our decision to surrender."

After the end of Taliban rule, Karzai agreed to send Taliban prisoners home, mostly to Pakistan and Iran. As for the Afghans involved in the Taliban movement, he wanted to bring them back into the system to hold jobs and return to a normal life.

Although the Taliban movement had been stopped, its members did not all turn in their weapons, as they had agreed. In fact, most Taliban and Al Qaeda fighters fled to the mountains and their hometowns after Mullah Mohammad Omar's surrender. More members continued to join Afghan warlords. Even Omar himself disappeared after the surrender, showing his apparent commitment to terrorism. The United States still hopes to find and punish former Taliban and Al Qaeda leaders, namely Omar and bin Laden. As long as U.S. troops remain in Afghanistan, they will be on the lookout for Omar and bin Laden.

6

After the Taliban

With the fall of the Taliban in early December 2001 came a need for an interim Afghanistan government. The question was: Who could head this temporary government? U.S. officials' first thought was to invite Zahir Shah, the former Afghan king, to take the job. Zahir, still living in Rome, had doubts about returning to Afghanistan, however. Although he had no health problems, he was not a young man—he was 87 years old when the United States approached him. In addition, he worried about security and safety issues upon his return to his homeland. Another likely candidate would be Burhanuddin Rabbani, who had been president of an interim Afghan government from 1992 to 1996, and the unofficial president until now.

Zahir suggested instead that Hamid Karzai, his longtime friend, who was well respected in the United States and Afghanistan, become

Although at first some wanted to bring Zahir Shah back to the throne, the former king wanted instead to have Karzai installed as the new leader of Afghanistan. Karzai is seen here in December 2001, talking with his advisors, soon after accepting the post of interim president.

the chairman of the interim government. Rabbani agreed with Zahir and wanted to see Karzai as chairman.

UN officials then organized a conference at which four Afghan factions would come together to discuss who should lead the interim government. One faction was the Northern Alliance, which consisted of Tajiks, Uzbeks, and Hazaras. The other three factions represented the largest ethnic group in Afghanistan, the Pushtuns. One represented Zahir Shah. A second, called Cyprus Process, consisted of politicians who had close relations with Iran. The third, called Peshawar Convention, consisted of Afghan exiles living in Pakistan.

On December 5, 2001, the very same day that Karzai suffered head injuries from the bomb that had been mistakenly dropped in Shawali Kowt, these Afghan factions reached an agreement after nine days of discussions in Bonn, Germany. Following Zahir's suggestion, Karzai would lead Afghanistan. Karzai had the support of not only all four Afghan factions, but also of the United States, Germany, Great Britain, and many other countries.

KEEPING AFGHANS SAFE

Even with support from around the world, Karzai and his 29-member executive council were faced with a difficult task. The people of Afghanistan were tired of warfare. For more than 20 years, war had occupied their lives. They wanted peace. For the next six months, they would look to Karzai to keep them safe. Many Afghans believed that Karzai was the person who could do this. It was unusual that a royalist Pushtun could be accepted by the Afghan people in the way that Karzai was after taking office, especially considering that Karzai was not even present at the Bonn meetings, since he had been in Kandahar fighting the last of the Taliban. However, the four Afghan factions present at the Bonn meetings, including the Northern Alliance, were in support of Karzai. One reason was that the people believed Karzai would not be governing out of greed or a desire to raise his tribal status. Karzai wanted good to come to *all* of Afghanistan's people.

Still, regardless of the support, the task he faced was enormous. The fear Afghans felt ran exceedingly deep. It had lasted decades. They were not safe walking down the street or even in their own homes. Bandits and warlords walked into civilians' homes and stopped cars on the highways, took what they wanted, recruited people for their missions, and terrorized others. One warlord, Abdul Rashid Dostum, an Uzbek, told the press he would boycott Karzai's government. A Pushtun spiritual leader, Sayed Ahmad Gailani, called the Bonn Conference "unjust."

To keep the people of Afghanistan safe, Karzai knew

In this December 22, 2001, photograph, the members of Karzai's new administration are seen taking the oath of office. Among them is Sima Samar (first row, second from left), the first woman to hold a major governmental position in Afghanistan.

extraordinary change would have to take place. He relied on the inspiration he had gained while studying the teachings and writings of Mohandas Gandhi. Like Gandhi, Karzai felt he could achieve his goals without violence. He told the Afghan people and the world that he planned to take away the guns and stop warlordism. He wanted to model Afghanistan after a country he greatly admired, Japan: a country that is both highly developed and respectful of traditional values.

SELECTING A CABINET AND LEADING A COUNTRY

As chairman of the interim government, Karzai oversaw five vice chairs: Sima Samar, minister of women's affairs; Muhammad Mohaqqeq, minister of planning; Shaker Kargar, minister of water and electricity; Hedayat Amin Arsala, minister of finance; and Mohammad Qassem Fahim, minister of defense.

The fact that a woman (Sima Samar) held a vice-chair position was a major step for Karzai and for the new Afghan government. Women's rights had long been suppressed under the Taliban. Afghanistan now had a woman in an influential government position, demonstrating that the nation was taking steps in the right direction. Although women had held government positions in Afghanistan's past, none had held such a prominent role. In addition to Sima Samar as minister of women's affairs, Karzai's cabinet included another woman, Suhaila Seddigi, as minister of public health.

Karzai took office on December 22, 2001. The interim government would last six months. During this time, an independent committee would prepare Afghanistan for a Loya Jirga. This assembly would meet to select a transitional government to take over after Karzai's six-month administration.

One of the first things Karzai did in office was to seek financial assistance from foreign countries. Afghanistan was in extreme financial hardship, and would not be able to rebuild without assistance. Building roads and schools, and establishing the banking, police and health-care systems all took money— money that Afghanistan did not have.

Karzai met with the Pakistani leader Pervez Musharraf to secure Pakistan's support for the reconstruction of Afghanistan. Then he traveled to the United States to meet with President George W. Bush—the first time in 39 years that an Afghan leader was officially welcomed in Washington, D.C. By the time he left, Karzai had been promised about $350 million in American aid. Turkey then agreed to lead an international force of about 5,000 peacekeeping troops to patrol Kabul, and Germany agreed to help set up Afghanistan's police force.

In his six months as chairman of the interim government of Afghanistan, Karzai did succeed in establishing some security in Afghanistan. Besides bringing in foreign aid and relief, Karzai began to reopen schools (which both males and females could now attend), establish banks, and remove weapons from

One of Karzai's first orders of business upon taking office was a trip to the United States to visit President George W. Bush, his partner in the overthrow of the Taliban regime. The two leaders in the war against terror are seen here walking together outside the White House.

warlords across the country. Various countries opened missions, dispensing aid in Kabul. The United Nations and the World Bank gave their full support to Afghanistan.

Due to Karzai's success in setting the stage for reconstruction, more than 200,000 refugees, many from neighboring Pakistan, made their way back home in the early months after he took office. Some were returning home after 20 years in exile. There was optimism in the air. Afghans wanted to be in their homeland to rebuild their country. When Karzai traveled to the United States, which he did frequently, he often spoke to crowds of Afghan Americans, hoping to persuade some of them to return to or visit Afghanistan. Some have taken up dual residency. They live for part of the year in the United States and spend the rest of the time in Afghanistan, where they can help in the reconstruction.

Security, however, was far from complete. Warlords continued to open fire on civilians. In the city of Gardiz, a warlord sent rockets into the middle of the city, killing and wounding innocent men, women, and children. It was clear that Karzai still had his hands full. He had to continue to try to stamp out warlordism and unite Afghans around a common goal for the future.

RETURN OF THE KING

In April 2002, the former king, Zahir Shah, returned to Afghanistan after 29 years in exile. Karzai flew to Rome, the former king's residence in exile, and made the trip back to Afghanistan with him. King Zahir Shah had no plans to try to take control of the government; he fully supported Karzai and what he was doing for Afghanistan. In interviews, Zahir praised Karzai's leadership abilities, character, and family.

Zahir's return to Kabul was met with a grand celebration by the people. As he left an Italian military plane, he was met with a red carpet flanked by Afghan children. Tribal elders and chiefs greeted Zahir as he made his way to his car. In Kabul, singers, dancers, and musicians performed in the streets. Onlookers crowded around to get a glimpse of the former king. The atmosphere was full of excitement and anticipation. Many Afghans associated the former king with a better way of life: a life before war and terrorism, a life filled with peace and happiness. To see him in person offered a glimmer of hope about what Afghanistan could be again.

After the festivities, Zahir retired to his new two-story home on a quiet street in Kabul. Like Karzai, Zahir continues to be heavily guarded at all times. Members of the International Security Assistance Force (ISAF) and U.S. troops patrol the

After being forced to spend almost 30 years outside his country, former King Zahir Shah finally returned to Afghanistan in April 2002. In this photograph taken in Italy a few months before Zahir Shah's dramatic homecoming, Karzai (left) kisses the hands of his former sovereign.

streets and stand guard at his home. With Zahir back in the country, he and Karzai are able to meet and discuss politics and the welfare of the country. Karzai makes it a point to visit him almost every day.

LOYA JIRGA

Six months passed quickly, and soon Karzai was nearing the end of his term as chief of the interim government. Not surprisingly, Karzai was once again elected the head of

Afghanistan. This time, the Loya Jirga, consisting of 1,500 delegates, elected him president. The delegates represented people of every group from around Afghanistan.

Karzai was elected to an 18-month term. Karzai originally selected three vice presidents: Haji Abdul Qadir, Mohammad Qassem Fahim, and Karim Khalili. Later, he appointed other vice presidents. When he announced the rest of the cabinet, he encountered some dissatisfaction, as some people opposed warlords being appointed to government positions. Karzai stood by his decisions, though.

Afghanistan was still primarily functioning under a system in which warlords ruled their separate territories. They each enlisted their own armies to defend their beliefs and interests. A great many rivalries existed among the warlords. Karzai hoped to put an end to warlordism with a unified government. To achieve this, he welcomed some of the well-known warlords into the government, in hopes of showing them that they could create a peaceful country by working together. He felt that warlords were better off in the government, where they had an opportunity to make changes for the better and go down in history as good people.

Upon taking office in June 2002, Karzai promised to keep Afghanistan under one leadership, bring all warlords under the Defense Ministry, and introduce what he called a "forceful Islamic government." He then told the people of Afghanistan that if he failed to keep his promises, he would submit his resignation.

Karzai is spending some of his time supervising the drafting of a constitution. The constitution will need to be approved by the Loya Jirga in October 2003. Nematullah Shahrani, one of the vice presidents appointed later, chairs the Constitutional Drafting Commission. Since beginning work on the constitution in the summer of 2002, much progress has been made. Shahrani completed a preliminary draft of the constitution in April 2003. The people of Afghanistan still need to decide if the constitution will create a presidential or a parliamentary republic. Karzai is helping to ensure that the constitution allows for freedom of the press and the formation of political parties. Shahrani will see that the appropriate laws are outlined in the constitution to honor these rights.

CHAPTER

7

Uncertain Times

Hamid Karzai made many promises upon taking office in mid-2002 for his second term. They would prove to be difficult to keep. In an effort to keep his word, he worked many hours in the presidential palace office, called *Gul Khana*, or "House of Flowers," located in Kabul. He often worked late into the evening, though he always tried to make time in the middle of each day to perform relaxation exercises. He would need to remain calm and focused as he tried to bring order to Afghanistan—especially in the latter half of 2002.

CIVILIANS KILLED IN BOMBING

Two events in early July 2002 led the Afghan people to start to doubt Karzai's ability to make their country safe again. First, an American military aircraft accidentally bombed an Afghan wedding party in the small village of Kakrakai in the Dehrawad district of the central province of Oruzgan. Reports said at least 40 people, many of them children, were killed instantly. Around 100 others were injured.

Why this tragedy happened is unclear. The American planes were there looking for Mullah Mohammad Omar, who escaped after the fall of the Taliban. Omar's hometown is Dehrawad, so the U.S. military planes had been patrolling the area for days. The Americans probably thought they were under attack when they heard the ceremonial firing of arms during the wedding party. As a result, they released their bombs.

Karzai made a public statement to the United States asking that this never happen again. He wanted to know that innocent civilians, like the many children who died in the bombing, would not be hurt in the future as the United States went after terrorists in Afghanistan. The United States expressed sympathy for the grieving families.

The bombing made some Afghans fear that Karzai was a weak leader. They worried that he gave in to the Americans too easily, allowing them to stay in the country searching for missing Taliban leaders. They questioned whether Americans should be allowed in Afghanistan if their presence could result in mistakes that killed children. Some Afghans thought Karzai was letting the United States dictate his actions. Others, however, felt he was doing the best he could. After all, they reasoned, the country was still engaged in a war of sorts against the ex-Taliban leaders.

TRAGEDY STRIKES AGAIN

Then, just one month after Karzai's new cabinet was sworn in, tragedy struck again. One of Karzai's three vice presidents, the warlord Haji Abdul Qadir, was assassinated. Qadir had arrived at work in Kabul and spent the morning scheduling appointments before heading out for lunch. He and his driver,

Despite the fact that Karzai's government had taken control of the country, Afghanistan still remained an unstable and sometimes violent place. In July 2002, one of Karzai's vice presidents, Haji Abdul Qadir, was assassinated. Here, military officials salute the late vice president's coffin.

who happened to be his son-in-law, got into their car and drove through the parking lot toward the front gates of the ministry. As they pulled through the gates, two gunmen jumped out from behind some bushes and started shooting at the car. Before driving away in a taxi, the gunmen put 48 bullets into the car. Qadir and his son-in-law were killed.

The attack left Karzai questioning the effectiveness of his ministry security. The International Security Assistance Force, located just a mile away, was not able to stop the shooting. Karzai had repeatedly asked for an expansion of the ISAF, but his requests had not been answered. After Qadir's assassination, however, Americans did call for additional help from the ISAF. They ordered troops sent to cities outside Kabul as well as the capital. This promise has yet to be fulfilled.

Later, witnesses to the shooting stated that the gunmen had been staking out the ministry for at least three hours, in full view of the ministry guards, who came under suspicion. Nine guards were brought in for questioning. The reasons behind Qadir's assassination are unknown. Most people believe it was some kind of conspiracy involving the ministry guards. It may have been terrorist-related, or it may have been a lashing out against Karzai and his government.

Qadir's death did not sit well with other warlords who had joined Karzai's government. They began to think that Karzai's hope of a unified government was impossible. In the government, they were not protected. As warlords in their own regions, though, they could enjoy the security of knowing that their personal armies would guard them. Karzai needed to return to the security issue he had dealt with his first time in office. He had to find a way to get more guns off the streets of Afghanistan.

Qadir's death left Afghanistan and Karzai scared. When the United States offered 70 special forces soldiers to replace Karzai's personal bodyguards, he readily accepted. To some Afghans, this move only increased concerns that Karzai was relying too heavily on the United States and giving it too much power over the country's future. Others saw his move as necessary protection to create a strong Afghan government. If Karzai were killed, Afghanistan's work toward independence and unity would be useless.

A BRUSH WITH DEATH

The country put its fears on hold long enough to celebrate its eighty-third Independence Day in August 2002. The day marked the country's independence from Great Britain in 1919. Security was extra tight, with the ISAF and Karzai's U.S. bodyguards patrolling continuously. Spirits remained high, though, and Afghans enjoyed the moment. Karzai and former King Zahir Shah both attended, and they made speeches expressing their good wishes for the future of Afghanistan and the Karzai government.

The celebratory mood lingering after Independence Day stopped abruptly a few weeks later. On a crowded shopping street in downtown Kabul on September 5, 2002, a bomb planted in a taxi exploded. At least 26 people were killed, and more than 150 people were injured. Afghan officials believed Al Qaeda was behind the attack, though it was not proven.

Less than four hours later, Karzai was shot at—though not harmed—while traveling in a car in his hometown, Kandahar. One of the assassin's bullets missed Karzai by mere inches. He was in Kandahar to attend the wedding of his youngest brother, Abdul Wali. In the car with Karzai was his close ally, Kandahar Governor Gul Agha Sherzai, who was slightly wounded. Sherzai was taken to a U.S. military base for medical attention. Driving in a car behind Karzai and Sherzai was Karzai's team of bodyguards.

The gunman was later identified as Abdul Rahman, a man who had recently been recruited for security at Sherzai's palace. Wearing his new uniform, Rahman stood near the gates of the governor's palace, waiting for an opportunity to open fire on Karzai. When Karzai drove out of the governor's compound, a young Afghan man approached the car in hopes of meeting Karzai. Karzai took a moment to open the car window and shake hands with the young man. Rahman saw his chance and shot four bullets at the car. Someone pushed Rahman onto the ground, and moments later, the U.S. special forces bodyguards were out of their car, returning fire. Three people were killed in the shooting: Rahman, the person who pushed Rahman to the ground, and one of the U.S. bodyguards. After the shooting, Karzai's bodyguards immediately drove him from the scene.

The assassination attempt did not surprise Karzai. He did not get too worried or frightened. To reporters he said, "I've been through this before. I've been hit three times at summits. Did that stop us from fighting? My father was assassinated by terrorists. Did that stop him from fighting against them? I will not stop. I'll continue."

Security issues continued in September 2002, when Afghan

Although Karzai was disturbed by the attempt on his life, he assured the public that he was prepared to deal with the danger and move on, in order to continue his work for Afghanistan. After the assassination attempt, bodyguards protected Karzai (right) at all times.

police stopped a truck headed for a U.S. air base near Kabul. The truck was full of explosives. Two days later, Al Qaeda forces shot rockets at a U.S. base in Khost. With each attack, Afghans feared for their country's safety and Karzai's ability to control it. Although the ISAF had promised to increase troops and expand its presence beyond Kabul, it still had only 5,000 troops, all of them in Kabul.

These incidents happened within days of the anniversary of the September 11 terrorist attacks in the United States. Around the world, people were apprehensive and frightened of additional terrorist attacks. Karzai traveled to the United States on September 10 to appear with President George W. Bush and many other world leaders at Ground Zero, the spot where the World Trade Center had once stood. A ceremony was held to remember the more than 3,000 people killed in the attacks.

WAR ON DRUGS

In addition to narrow escapes from assassins and trying to piece a country back together again, Karzai had another problem to deal with—illegal drugs. The statistics on drugs in Afghanistan are staggering. The country is the world's biggest producer of opium poppies, the raw ingredient of heroin. More than 90 percent of the heroin sold in Europe comes from Afghanistan. Karzai hopes to stop the production of poppies by showing farmers that there are alternative crops.

While the Taliban controlled Afghanistan, they banned the production of poppy. As a result, very little poppy was grown in 2001. Once the Taliban were defeated, though, farmers returned to poppy crops because they bring in huge amounts of money—about eight times more per hectare (about 2.5 acres) than wheat. Neighboring countries buy poppy at top dollar. In 2002, Afghanistan produced 3,400 tons of poppy.

Karzai extended the ban on poppy production after the Taliban fell, but his government has been unable to enforce it. The Taliban used force to direct poppy production; Karzai's government does not use force, and its ban is being ignored. In part, this is because growing poppy does not require much work, just a small amount of water and labor. A crop that needs little water is a good thing after four years of extreme drought. Very few crops are able to grow as easily as poppy plants in such arid soil. In another attempt to stop poppy production, Karzai's government paid farmers to destroy their poppy fields. This, however, cost a great deal of money, which is in short supply.

The need to stop the drug trade is heightened because of the HIV/AIDS infection rate in Central Asia, which is increasing at the fastest pace in the world. The United Nations has reported a direct link between the Afghan drug trade and the rapid increase of HIV/AIDS in Central Asia.

Researchers are trying to find ways to turn around Afghanistan's drug problem. Finding alternative crops is essential. The most likely crops to benefit Afghan farmers will be fruits and nuts—almonds, for example. More than 60 varieties of almonds are grown in Afghanistan. If people can protect and develop this crop, exports could greatly increase. To make this happen, though, orchards will need to be replanted, since many died out from the years of drought. This takes an enormous amount of time.

Meanwhile, some relief has helped farmers. The International Center for Agricultural Research in the Dry Areas sent 3,500 tons of high-quality wheat seed to Afghan farmers in 2002. They received the wheat in time for the spring. The wheat crops will help feed hungry Afghans and may also cut down on part of the poppy production.

ANOTHER CLOSE CALL

On November 24, 2002, Karzai was almost killed again. Bokan Akram Khorani, a 22-year-old Iraqi Kurd, was sent on a suicide mission. Khorani had trained in Pakistan-occupied Kashmir to perform the mission for the Taliban. His orders were to assassinate Karzai as he returned to Afghanistan from a trip to the United States. As it turned out, Khorani arrived too late to assassinate Karzai.

Instead, Khorani tried to use the Taliban's plan against Defense Minister Mohammad Qassem Fahim. For days, he watched Fahim's neighborhood. This alerted the police, who had seen Khorani cross into the country from Pakistan. Security forces arrested Khorani, found with 18 pounds of explosives strapped to his body, before he could get to Fahim. Once in custody, Khorani told officials in reference to the suicide mission, it "would be an honor to succeed in the operation."

8

Rebuilding Afghanistan

At the start of 2003, a year after the defeat of the Taliban, Afghanistan still faced problems. Hamid Karzai struggled to extend his power outside the capital city of Kabul. Factional fighting continued to rage across the country. Warlords had gained power, and the Pushtun tribes in the east and south felt left out of the Karzai government.

To try to compensate for the Pushtuns' unhappiness, Defense Minister Fahim announced that he would reorganize his ministry in hopes of making it more ethnically balanced. In trying to end warlordism, which has prevailed since 1989 when the Soviet Union ended its occupation, Karzai stated that he would demobilize the militias before mid-2004, when national elections are expected to take place. His plan, called DDR (demilitarization, demobilization, and reintegration), could help bring peace to Afghanistan. Karzai said he

Karzai's plan for Afghanistan is known as DDR—demilitarization, demobilization, and reintegration. In this January 2002 photograph, he is seen on a large TV screen as he addresses the International Conference on Reconstruction Assistance to Afghanistan (which met in Tokyo) with an outline of his plan.

planned to bring some of the warlords' militia soldiers into the new Afghanistan army and others into civilian jobs. Few people believe the warlords will easily give up the estimated 8 million guns they have in circulation. The process will be long, tedious, and expensive (estimates run around $140 million).

Whether Karzai's plans will succeed is yet to be seen. When Karzai undertook similar efforts to disband militias in 2002, the results were disheartening: The more powerful militias simply forced smaller militias to hand their weapons over to them. This did nothing more than make the large militias even more powerful.

One positive change is that the numbers of remaining Taliban and Al Qaeda supporters hiding near the Pakistan border are dwindling. Most have to move around, since they have few allies in either Afghanistan or Pakistan. When supporters of the Taliban and Al Qaeda try to ship them weapons, the shipments are usually intercepted by Afghan officials and handed over to the Karzai government.

FOREIGN AID

Rebuilding a country after 23 years of war takes a lot of money and resources. In January 2002, nations around the world had promised $4.5 billion in foreign aid to Afghanistan to be distributed over five years. The World Bank estimates this figure is only about half of what it will actually cost to rebuild Afghanistan. Most of the $4.5 billion is yet to be seen. Of the money coming in, most is being spent to bring refugees home. The slow distribution of the money is making it difficult for Karzai and his government to move forward with reconstruction.

Iran has been a huge supporter of Afghanistan. The two nations have long kept close ties. Most of Afghanistan's imports come by way of Iran. It promised $560 million in aid and has started repairing the highway that runs from Herat, Afghanistan, into Iran. In addition, it set up 2,000 Iranian university scholarships for Afghan students.

In September 2002, the United States promised $80 million, Japan $50 million, and Saudi Arabia $50 million to aid in the reconstruction of Afghanistan's highways. With an improved transportation system, much of which had been destroyed during the two decades of war, Afghanistan is beginning to regain its trade businesses. Karzai has also made a point of working out trade deals with other countries, such as India and Iran. By increasing imports and exports, Karzai hopes to strengthen Afghanistan's economy.

Other international aid has gone into rebuilding Kabul. Besides new businesses, hotels have begun to appear there. Afghanistan is not in a position to draw tourists, but it does need to house and feed large numbers of aid workers, journalists, and government officials. To keep patrons safe, armed guards stand outside most of the hotels and restaurants in Kabul.

RETURNING REFUGEES

Although Afghanistan continues to face problems, such as security issues and drugs, Afghans still have hope for their country's future under Karzai's leadership. Afghan refugees from around the world have gradually been returning since Karzai became president. By March 2003, about 2 million refugees had already returned to Afghanistan from camps in Pakistan and Iran. This was the largest human migration since the formation of Bangladesh in 1971. Hundreds of thousands more displaced Afghans—people forced to leave their homes, but able to remain in their country—made their way back to their homes. Karzai would like to see the return of all Afghan refugees and displaced people. It is a good sign that people are returning to the country upon seeing the effects of Karzai's government.

Most refugees return to northern Afghanistan. Upon arrival, they discover that housing problems exist. As more and more people return, the cities have grown more crowded. Coming home to Kabul is nearly impossible, since it is in no shape to house the returning refugees. Most of the city remains in ruins. Overflowing sewers leave the air unbearable. There are frequent blackouts and little clean water. It will take much money to rebuild the city. People end up living in worse conditions in Afghanistan than they had in refugee camps.

One of the biggest problems Karzai has faced has been the return of refugees from outside Afghanistan, which has created a massive influx of people and has caused housing problems. Despite these difficulties, Karzai has expressed a desire to see all refugees, like this man seen praying for the safe return of his family, come home.

They come home and find themselves forced to live in temporary shelters, often without clean water and basic necessities, due to a lack of housing.

Those who lived in villages outside Kabul before they left for Pakistan are not much better off. Robbers stripped many homes of their possessions while refugees were out of the country. Families came home to find their houses empty or even burned to the ground. Even if refugees did find their homes still standing and their possessions intact, four years of drought had left most farmland unworkable and most orchards in shambles. Three-quarters of Afghanistan's livestock died during the drought. Areas where rivers once flowed have become a landscape of dried, cracked dirt.

Although huge numbers of refugees have returned, there are still millions more to come home. An estimated 2 million refugees are still in Iran, with 1.5 million in Pakistan. Karzai is working on improving the living conditions for all Afghans to persuade people to return.

In recognition of Karzai's work to bring home refugees, he was presented with a Freedom Award by the International Rescue Committee (IRC) in November 2002. The IRC is a global humanitarian aid organization that has assisted Afghan refugees since 1980. The IRC presented the award to Karzai at a dinner in Manhattan, New York. About 800 political and IRC supporters attended the benefit.

The award acknowledged Karzai's leadership and courage as he helped his people move toward peace and freedom. The president of the IRC, Dr. George Rupp, said, "[W]e especially appreciate President Karzai's determination to help his people return home after their long exile." Upon accepting the award, Karzai said that it "not only lifts my spirit further to continue to struggle for freedom, but this award actually acknowledges the love for freedom of the Afghan people, whom the IRC has served for many years."

EDUCATION

Getting Afghan children to school remains a huge priority for Karzai. When the Soviets invaded Afghanistan more than 20 years ago, 5 million Afghans left the country. Of those who have come back, many are uneducated. During their stay in refugee camps, they did not receive schooling. When the Taliban controlled Afghanistan, they did not allow females to go to school after age eight. Boys who did attend school under the Taliban learned almost exclusively about Islam. Large numbers of Afghan children and even adults today have had little or no education.

The future of Afghanistan depends on its children's education. Since Karzai took office, around 2 million Afghan boys and one million Afghan girls returned to school, exceeding expectations. The United Nations had predicted that only about 1.5 million children would return so quickly.

In March 2002, Karzai attended a ceremony at Amani High School in Kabul. Although Amani High School is a boys' school, girls from neighboring schools also attended. The ceremony marked the first day of the 2002 school year, which runs from March to December in most of Afghanistan. In the warmer climate of eastern and southern Afghanistan, schools are open from September to June. About 3.3 million children finished the school year following the fall of the Taliban.

The students faced rough conditions. There were textbook and classroom shortages, even though the United States had donated some 4 million textbooks by the start of the school year and Japan had supplied 60 percent of the financial aid given to Afghanistan for education. Basic supplies such as chalk, paper, and blackboards were also in great demand. In some areas, students had to attend classes in shifts to accommodate too many students for too few classrooms. Private homes, mosque courtyards, and tents became makeshift schools in rural areas where bombs had destroyed schools.

Another problem facing schoolchildren is poor nutrition and the lack of adequate food. In February 2003, Karzai helped distribute 10,000 fortified high-energy biscuits that had been donated by India to students at Amani High School. India's aid to Afghanistan is helping to feed the children in rural areas where food is scarce. India's hope is that the children will be better able to concentrate on their lessons if they don't feel the effects of hunger. Besides feeding the children, the biscuits have also helped boost school attendance.

Despite the problems, Karzai continues to urge parents to send their children back to school. Before the opening of the 2002 school year, religious leaders at mosques around the

One of the most promising changes that has come into effect under Karzai's leadership has been the reopening of schools and a renewed emphasis on education for Afghan children. Under the Taliban, education had been extremely restricted, and girls were not allowed to attend school after age eight.

country talked to parents about the importance of educating their children. They emphasized that the welfare of the country depends on raising future doctors, teachers, scientists, and agriculturists.

At the end of the 2002 school year, several schools for girls outside Kabul were burned. Karzai said, "The people who destroyed and burned those schools are our enemies. They want the nation to be poor and needy." Karzai has different ideas. He wants the nation to be wealthy and independent.

For the 2003 school year, another one million students were estimated to join the 3.3 million children already in school. The Afghanistan Education Ministry plans to hand out another 13.9 million donated textbooks and deliver another 1.5 million tables and chairs. The Education Ministry also hopes to train additional teachers in every province.

TECHNOLOGY AND THE ARTS

Afghanistan activated its first Internet domain—".af"—in March 2003. The Taliban had previously banned the use of the Internet. Setting up an Internet domain is a huge technological step for Afghanistan. Even so, most Afghans are not yet able to make much use of their new domain, since the average person in Kabul earns less than a dollar a day and cannot afford a computer.

Gradually, art and culture are returning to Afghanistan. Karzai saw the reopening of the Kabul Art Gallery and the Kabul School of Music, both of which had been shut down during the Taliban rule. He hopes to see Afghan artifacts on display at Musée Guimet in Paris, France, returned to the Kabul Museum. The Olympia Gold Gym opened in November 2002 in a middle-class area of Kabul. Young people crowd into the gym to exercise and to socialize with their peers.

Rebuilding Kabul also entails rehabilitating and preserving the historic walls that grace its borders. One wall in particular, called Zanborak Shah, was built more than 1,800 years ago and could eventualiy be a major tourist attraction. Efforts to restore the city's walls are under way.

WOMEN'S RIGHTS

Women have not always been treated as equal citizens in Afghanistan. In part, this has to do with the nation's Muslim culture, in which men play an important role in social life. They make most decisions and lay down the rules. Women take care of the home and family.

Although Muslim culture may hold strict codes of conduct for women, Afghan women suffered extreme hardship that went far beyond religious rules under the Taliban. They could not go to school, they could not be seen in public without a male relative, and they had to be covered from head to toe in a traditional burqa. Although the burqa has a small netted opening through which women can see, it still obstructs their vision. Women cannot see to the sides without turning their heads. It is very difficult to navigate while wearing the burqa. Many women have been killed crossing streets because they could not see oncoming cars.

Though women have gained rights under the Karzai government, they still do not enjoy fully equal treatment. Families in rural areas who try to send their girls to school are sometimes threatened. Because the ISAF is absent outside of Kabul, women in rural areas continue to face discrimination from armed civilians. Some of these men still believe in the severe Taliban laws and take the law into their own hands, punishing women for not following the old rules.

Many women, such as First Lady Zinat Karzai, fear being kidnapped. It was fairly common during Taliban rule for men to enter homes looking for young girls to kidnap. Their bodies would often be dumped in the family's front yard after they had been raped repeatedly.

Some women feel that Karzai needs to take a stand and allow his wife out into the public eye. Many people would like

In complete contradiction to the old Taliban system, women in Afghanistan today are not only permitted to move freely in society, but are taking part in the political process. These women were delegates to the Loya Jirga that was held in June 2002.

to have Zinat Karzai be a role model, not an invisible first lady. They would like to see Hamid Karzai follow in the footsteps of King Aman Allah, who, in 1919, made great strides toward the independence of Afghan women. At that time, Afghanistan was breaking free from British rule. For the 1919 Independence Day celebration, Aman Allah ordered all government officials to bring their wives. His wife, Queen Soraya, and the government officials' wives all attended in formal attire. None wore a burqa. These bold acts showed Afghanistan a new government and more liberal rules. People today want the same from Hamid and Zinat Karzai.

In one report, Zinat Karzai stated that she hoped to work toward improving women's rights in Afghanistan. She does not think women should wear burqas. She chooses not to wear one herself. Instead, she wraps a white scarf around her hair. Zinat also wants to return to her gynecology practice, which she stopped after Karzai's father was assassinated. Afghanistan needs good doctors, and Zinat hopes to help fill that need one day soon.

The good news is that women are returning to the University of Kabul. In addition, women in urban areas now have better access to health care and employment. Under the Taliban, women were often turned away from health care. Because women could not leave the house without a male escort, some women, including widows and unmarried women, had no way to get to health-care facilities. Another positive change can be found in Afghanistan's government. Some 200 women took part in the Loya Jirga—the highest number seen in any Loya Jirga in Afghanistan's history. The Ministry of Women's Affairs is also taking bold strides to advance women's rights.

9

Karzai Brings Hope – and Skepticism

There has never been an official census in Afghanistan, so population estimates are just that—estimates. Researchers guess that there are 16 million to 28 million people living in Afghanistan. It is by no means a wealthy country. The average income is less than $500 a year. Almost two-thirds of the population cannot read or write. President Hamid Karzai is hoping to turn these numbers around and bring economic relief to Afghanistan.

A new national currency, called the afghani, was successfully introduced at the start of 2003. Before, at least four different currencies cycled through Afghanistan. Some Afghan warlords even printed their own money. In October 2002, Karzai's government began exchanging old currency for the new afghani. The deadline for exchanging money was January 2, 2003. Establishing the afghani created a less confusing and more dependable financial system.

New road construction totaling some 3,750 miles (6,035 kilometers), the rebuilding of Kabul and other cities, and irrigation projects should create tens of thousands of new jobs for the unemployed in Afghanistan. Average wages will run about two U.S. dollars a day.

NATIONAL ARMY

One of Karzai's most ambitious plans for Afghanistan is to establish a 70,000-member national army by the end of 2003. At present, there are only about 3,000 men in the army. Some reports state that as many as half of these soldiers have already deserted due to low pay and poor housing. Karzai continues to work hard to increase the numbers. He meets with foreign leaders to discuss the importance of a national army in Afghanistan and how it could help to bring independence to a country that currently has to rely on the armies of other countries.

Karzai is trying to break up private militias throughout the country. Although he declared these militias illegal and their weapons national property, warlords continue armed factional fighting over territorial, ethnic, and political disputes outside of Kabul. Little by little, Karzai is trying to get their weapons turned over to the government. There are about 100 militia members for every one national army member, however. In early December 2002, fighting broke out in the western province of Herat. The U.S. military sent in soldiers to launch a B-52 bomb attack, which left at least 27 people dead or injured. Karzai is trying to persuade militia members to join the national army. If everyone would work on the same side, he argues, Afghanistan might at last see an end to the violence.

Karzai also wants to weed out corrupt officials — usually warlords — in government positions. Without well-trained police officers, the country cannot achieve its goals of peace and unity. In one instance where Afghan officials were

Karzai hopes to protect his nation and government by rebuilding the Afghan military, which has been decimated in recent years by financial problems. Karzai (front, at center) is seen here inspecting the 1st Battalion of the Afghan National Guard in July 2002.

working without the best interests of the country in mind, the Kabul police began firing at college students during a demonstration against poor university conditions. Two students were killed. Karzai hopes to improve the situation. In December 2002, he dismissed 29 warlord officials from government positions. Some were fired because of their direct involvement in the illegal poppy trade. Karzai said that warlords were forbidden to have both political and military roles in the government. Some warlords have complied with Karzai's orders and chosen either a military or political role. Others have ignored him.

Karzai traveled to Oslo, Norway, where he met with Kristin Krohn Devold, Norwegian defense minister, to ask for assistance in establishing a national army. As more people join the national army, those soldiers and pilots will need training. Karzai hopes that Norway, working in a unit under the International Security Assistance Force, will help with this training. Norway's special operation forces have been working alongside American soldiers in Afghanistan. Turkey, too, along with numerous other countries, plans to provide training facilities for Afghan soldiers and pilots in military training camps in Turkey.

In March 2003, Karzai was honored to introduce the first two brigades of the Afghan army. The brigades, comprised of about 2,000 men each, had just completed their ten-week training course. At the ceremony, Karzai told the soldiers to help rebuild their country and paid tribute to those who had died doing so.

A 70,000-member unified army would mean that Afghanistan could have dependable security throughout the country. People could depend on a determined set of laws and consequences. The ceremony activating the two brigades told Afghanistan and the world that the country was moving forward with its military plans. The national army became an officially established organization.

SUPPORT FROM FOREIGN COUNTRIES

In another effort to bring peace to Afghanistan, Karzai attended a conference to strengthen relations with neighbors in December 2002. With him were foreign ministers from China, Iran, Pakistan, Tajikistan, Turkmenistan, and Uzbekistan. The countries worked to develop an agreement that promised respect and understanding between them. By strengthening relations among neighbors, Karzai and other leaders hope to build a region free of terrorism and extremist beliefs.

Karzai met with U.S. President George W. Bush in February 2003. When addressing Bush and Congress, Karzai requested additional aid. He did not want to be forgotten as the United States focused on the war with Iraq, which began later in the month. Karzai went on to highlight accomplishments since the Taliban had been ousted. Karzai's reception, however, was not warm. He got a stern lecture from U.S. senators, who accused him of sugarcoating Afghanistan's problems. Karzai took offense to these allegations. President Bush later called Karzai to apologize for the senators' remarks.

Despite the scolding Karzai received, he did leave his meeting with promises of U.S. aid in areas of agriculture, education, health, and transportation. Bush also assured Karzai that the 10,000 American troops in Afghanistan would continue to work toward preventing terrorism and helping to build Afghanistan's national army.

In March 2003, working to further repair relations with Pakistan, Afghanistan agreed to release nearly 900 Pakistani prisoners who had fought with the Taliban. Most of the prisoners were being held in northern Afghanistan in the town of Shibarghan. Although Pakistan had supported the Taliban for many years, it joined the United States in trying to remove the Taliban after the September 11 attacks.

Karzai was scheduled to be the guest of honor at the Pakistan National Parade Day in March 2003. Pakistanis canceled the parade because of the impending U.S. war in Iraq. Karzai still met with Pakistan President Pervez Musharraf and Prime Minister Zafarullah Khan Jamali to discuss Karzai's policy of noninterference from neighboring countries.

The United States and Norway have additional plans to aid Afghanistan over a three-year period: They will build a bridge over the river separating Afghanistan from Tajikistan, restore irrigation and water management systems, build or fix existing schools, train new teachers, and build or repair existing health-care systems.

THE FUTURE OF KARZAI AND AFGHANISTAN

Hamid Karzai has accomplished much in his position as the leader of Afghanistan. He has brought millions of Afghans back to their homeland after years of living outside the country as refugees. He has reopened schools and museums, and brought culture back to a country that had been void of such luxuries under harsh Taliban rule. The Karzai government has confiscated 175,000 explosives found hidden in Kabul.

Karzai has a special way of connecting with the people of Afghanistan. When he makes speeches around the country, he is sure to alternate between the Pashtu and Dari languages, so as to address everyone. He steers clear of labels like "Tajik" or "Uzbek" or "Pushtun." Instead, he uses the term "Afghan," further stressing his desire for unity among the people. He shares with Afghans his beliefs of nonviolence and tolerance of all people.

Yet Karzai also faces a great many challenges. Warlords still dominate the rural areas of Afghanistan. As long as they do, the Karzai government will be limited. Economic aid from foreign countries, especially from the United States after it took up its war in Iraq, became less dependable. Karzai also faces criticism of being too dependent on the

In the aftermath of the Taliban's brutal reign and the powerful military action required to remove the regime, much of Afghanistan was left in rubble. To inspire his people and raise hopes for a brighter future, Karzai ordered a one-day mass cleaning campaign. The sign behind these workers reads, "Rise up, Afghanistan."

United States for international aid and protection. Some Afghans maintain that the West—not Karzai—controls Afghanistan.

Karzai has made it clear that he will continue his quest to bring peace and freedom to Afghanistan as long as he is living. With the support of his country and the world, and with his continued personal commitment and focused effort, perhaps he will, over time, see his dream come true.

1200s Hazara ethnic group settles in central Afghanistan.

Mid-1700s King Ahmed Shah Durrani establishes the city of Kandahar.

1800s Persia, Great Britain, and Russia all fight for control of Afghanistan.

Early 1900s Great Britain claims control of Afghanistan.

1919 Shah Aman Allah wins independence for Afghanistan; moves country toward modernization.

1930 King Nadir Shah passes a new constitution, which remains in place for 34 years.

1933 King Nadir Shah is assassinated; his son Zahir Shah becomes king and rules until 1973.

1957 Hamid Karzai is born on December 24 in Kandahar.

1964 King Zahir Shah signs a new liberal constitution, creating a parliamentary democracy with a constitutional monarchy.

1973 Mohammad Daoud overthrows his cousin, King Zahir Shah, and forces Zahir into exile in Rome, Italy; Daoud declares Afghanistan a republic on July 17.

Mid-1970s The People's Democratic Party of Afghanistan (PDPA), a Communist organization, gains power in Afghanistan.

1976 Hamid Karzai travels to India and starts college.

1978 The PDPA kills Daoud during the Saur (April) Revolution, declaring Afghanistan the Democratic Republic of Afghanistan.

Late 1970s Afghan Communists and Soviets kill or imprison many Afghan leaders; Abdul Ahad Karzai (Hamid's father) is imprisoned.

1979 The Soviets' Red army secures Kabul on December 26; the Soviet occupation lasts ten years.

1981 Abdul Ahad Karzai is released from prison; moves family to Quetta, Pakistan, to escape the Communists.

CHRONOLOGY

1982 Hamid Karzai earns a master's degree from Himachal Pradesh University in Shimla, India; rejoins his father and family, still living in exile in Quetta, Pakistan; becomes the director of operations of the Afghan National Liberation Front, based in Peshawar, Pakistan.

Early 1980s Hamid Karzai supports a newly forming Afghan resistance movement of fighters called the mujahideen.

1988 In April, Afghanistan, Soviet Union, Pakistan, and the United States meet in Geneva, Switzerland; reach agreement on a cease-fire and on the withdrawal of Soviet troops from Afghanistan; troops begin withdrawal in May.

1989 In February, the remaining Soviet troops withdraw; the Soviet occupation is over.

1992 In April, the mujahideen, who had been ruling the countryside, overthrow Sayid Mohammed Najibullah, the Communist president; Karzai returns to Afghanistan to serve as deputy foreign minister under the mujahideen government; Afghanistan becomes an Islamic state (church and religious leaders control the government's decisions); the Northern Alliance leader, Burhanuddin Rabbani, becomes president of interim government (through 1996).

1994 Karzai resigns his post as deputy foreign minister and returns to Pakistan; anarchy has taken over much of Afghanistan.

1999 Hamid's father, Abdul Ahad Karzai, is assassinated.

2001 In March, the Taliban destroy two nearly 2,000-year-old Buddha statues in central Afghanistan; on September 11, more than 3,000 people die in terrorist attacks in the United States, ordered by Osama bin Laden; in early October, Karzai returns to Afghanistan to fight the Taliban; U.S. President George W. Bush orders air strikes on Afghanistan to remove the Taliban and Al Qaeda; on November 13, the Northern Alliance reclaims Kabul from the Taliban; on December 5, Karzai meets with remaining Taliban officials, who deliver their surrender; on December 22, Karzai takes office as leader of a six-month interim government for Afghanistan.

2002 Karzai is elected president of Afghanistan for an 18-month term; in July, a U.S. military aircraft accidentally bombs an Afghan wedding party in Kakrakai; warlord Haji Abdul Qadir, one of Karzai's three vice presidents, is assassinated; in September, a car bomb explodes in Kabul; four hours, later an assassination attempt is made on Karzai; in October, Karzai's government begins exchanging old currency for the new afghani; in November, Karzai is presented with a Freedom Award by the International Rescue Committee (IRC); on November 24, Karzai escapes a Taliban-ordered assassination attempt.

2003 By March, about 2 million refugees have returned to Afghanistan; hundreds of thousands more displaced Afghans also have returned home; in March, Afghanistan activates its first Internet domain ".af."; Karzai introduces the first two brigades of the Afghan army.

Ali, Sharifah Enayat. *Cultures of the World: Afghanistan.* New York: Marshall Cavendish, 1995.

Grazda, Edward. *Afghanistan Diary, 1992–2000.* New York: PowerHouse Books, 2000.

"The Rebirth of a Nation: Afghanistan." *The Economist,* January 11, 2003, vol. 366.

Tanner, Stephen. *Afghanistan: A Military History From Alexander the Great to the Fall of the Taliban.* Cambridge, MA: Da Capo Press, 2002.

Tyson, Ann Scott. "Red Carpet Leads Back to a Nation in Tatters." *Christian Science Monitor,* January 31, 2002.

WEB SITES

Access Afghanistan
www.accessafghanistan.com

Afghan Info Center
www.afghan-info.com

Akhtar, Humayun. "Karzai—A Hero in the Making?"
www.pakistanlink.com

"His Excellency Hamid Karzai: President of Afghanistan." June 7, 2002,
www.achievement.org

Land of the Afghans: History Through Times
www.afghanland.com

McGirk, Tim. "The Lone Man Without a Gun."
www.time.com

page:

ANNE M. TODD lives in Prior Lake, Minnesota, with her husband, Sean, and two sons, Spencer and William. She received a Bachelor of Arts degree in English and American Indian Studies from the University of Minnesota. She has written a number of children's books, including biographies about American Indians and informative books about American history.

ARTHUR M. SCHLESINGER, JR. is the leading American historian of our time. He won the Pulitzer Prize for his book *The Age of Jackson* (1945) and again for a chronicle of the Kennedy administration, *A Thousand Days* (1965), which also won the National Book Award. Professor Schlesinger is the Albert Schweitzer Professor of the Humanities at the City University of New York and has been involved in several other Chelsea House projects, including the series REVOLUTIONARY WAR LEADERS, COLONIAL LEADERS, and YOUR GOVERNMENT.